CHOOSE TO BE A LEADER OTHERS WOULD WANT TO FOLLOW

How to Lead with Heart and Purpose

BY

DR. JOHANNA PAGONIS

Paperback ISBN 978-1-7771561-0-7
eBook ISBN 978-1-7771561-1-4

Publisher: Johanna Pagonis
Editor: Laura Neilson Bonikowsky
Cover design: Johanna Pagonis
Interior design: ebookpbook.com

PREFACE

I welcome feedback and comments from anyone who has invested their time in reading my work. You can contact me through:

Website: https://sinogapsolutions.com
LinkedIn: linkedin.com/company/sinogapsolutions
Twitter: https://twitter.com/Sinogap
Facebook: https://www.facebook.com/sinogapsolutions

This is a work of non-fiction. Pseudonyms have been used to protect the anonymity of my research participants. Any resemblance to persons living or dead is a coincidence and unintentional.

DEDICATION

To my husband Jerry, my constant and steadfast support in the pursuit of my ambitious dreams, who brags about my accomplishments. Thank you for listening to my ideas and always having faith in me. You are the anchor of my kite, keeping me safely connected to the earth as I soar to new heights.

"I inherently believe what drives people to excellence is igniting their passion through their purpose."
Dr. Johanna Pagonis

Contents

A Note from Johanna

When I became a manager, I had no idea what it truly meant to be a leader. Over the years, I had developed a lot of confidence as a technically skilled employee, but that confidence did not transition smoothly when I became a manager. Although my organization had developed an onboarding program for new employees to ease them into their new role and acclimate them to the culture, there wasn't one for managers. Neither was there much support for learning how to be a manager. "Sink or swim" and "trial by fire" are some of the metaphors that come to mind when I reflect on how I learned to be a manager.

There was no denying I was struggling when I almost ran over a pedestrian on my way home one day, because I was absorbed in thought about how I was going to manage a member on my team who appeared to enjoy tormenting me with his entitled and crude behaviour. The reality is, most people learn how to be a manager in those conditions. I believe that managers are the linchpin to organizational success and employee engagement. We have to do a better job of equipping individuals with the skills that will help them attain organizational goals while motivating others.

I was fortunate enough in my career to have worked for some amazing managers who were also inspiring leaders. But how does someone become a competent manager and a confident leader? Are they born with that ability or do they learn it? Is there a difference between manager and leader? Do individuals have to be good at both?

To discover the answers to my questions I decided to go back to school to pursue a PhD while still working full-time as a manager for the Government of Alberta. I guess you can say I am a glutton for punishment, but I do have a passion for research and there is something to say about evidence-based data that is not solely based on one's experience. There is not a lot of research on how organizations develop managers. There are many studies on how to develop human resources. However, few of them have looked into how organizations develop their managers and how that process affects managers' performance. This gap is surprising considering the training industry is a 3-billion-dollar money-making machine.

From my own review of the research, I discovered many organizations take a one-size-fits-all approach to managerial development regardless of a manager's experience, level of confidence, and ability. Take a moment to think about your training and development. Did you attend the same training as your colleagues and somehow you were supposed to come back as a fully competent and capable leader? We believe knowledge is ready-to-wear and therefore there is little attention paid to how you will transfer your newly acquired knowledge to your workplace. Most of the time we return to work the next day without giving a second thought to what we just learned. How can we? We now have 300 e-mails to read and respond to, a project deadline looming over our heads and three of our staff standing outside the door wanting support.

The managers in my research study told me that roughly 90% of how they learned to do their job came from doing the job. The other 10% came from training. This is true in general, not only for managerial development. Why do we keep sending people to training thinking it will actually make a difference? I am not saying we shut down post-secondary institutions and deplete our training budgets, but for knowledge gained from a course to be transferred to the workplace, there must be further learning and practice so new knowledge can be ready to use in a range of workplace contexts.[1]

To assume managers will figure out on their own how to support their own workplace learning is not realistic. In today's workplace, managers are overburdened. This results in being overworked and conducting many tasks superficially.[2] The resulting chaotic nature of a manager's work environment makes the job very complex and challenging. The philosophy of "learn as you go" becomes increasingly difficult to tolerate, because managers are required to balance the immediate demands of the organization against the needs of their employees.[3]

Donald A. Schön referred to the chaotic nature of a manager's work environment as the "swampy lowland" where situations are confusing messes.[4] Unfortunately, real-life problem-solving does not rely on a decision-making model based on choosing a course of action from an existing playbook, but rather based on information that is incomplete, ambiguous, and shifting. Learning at work is becoming a key focus of development in the field of management and is a central concern for organizations.[5] Managers need a climate where continuous learning is not only supported, but is embedded in workplace culture as well. Organizations must address that need.

My professor told me once that a scholar's gift is the ability to integrate concepts from different theories in a cohesive way. This book is my attempt to do just that. I intend to connect the dots for you by applying some inspirational works of others in a way that demonstrates how different concepts can work together to inform our practice as managers and leaders. My goal for this book is that people, especially leaders in top ranks, will be motivated to create a workplace environment where managers are supported and encouraged to embrace their vulnerability.

This book is divided into three parts. The first explores the workplace as an enriched landscape for managerial learning and leadership development. I will explain informal learning and how people learn from experience. The second part focuses mainly on the results of my research. Specifically, I will answer three questions:

- What are managers learning in the workplace.
- How are managers learning in the workplace?
- What are the workplace factors that affect someone's ability to learn in the workplace?

The third part of this book provides organizations with recommendations of how to develop a plan for learning at work that has meaning and serves a purpose. Throughout my career, I have promoted leadership and education; for me they go hand-in-hand, and I have continually explored avenues of learning that are embedded in the workplace. When the breadth of research came up short, I decided to pursue a PhD in a topic that would directly benefit others. My personal vision is to support leaders in investing in workplace learning strategies that go beyond normative training practices, so their companies can evolve to become true learning organizations.

A critical element in learning is self-reflection, which leads to improved performance. How can someone improve their performance if they do not have time to reflect on what worked well and what did not? Therefore, I have written this book in a format that will give you the gift of time to reflect to help you uncover your beliefs about management, leadership, and learning. Below are four questions—you can use the blank pages at the end of this chapter to answer them if, like me, you like to write down your thoughts.

Time to Reflect:
1. **What does a manager do?**
2. **What does a leader do?**
3. **How does someone learn to become a manager?**
4. **What do you believe about leadership?**

CHECKING OUR BIASES AT THE DOOR

I used to believe that being a manager and a leader were one and the same. It was only when I conducted my own research that my belief system was challenged. The research participants in my PhD study discussed how they faced multiple dilemmas. They talked about the importance of considering the larger system they worked within, while at the same time considering their employees' needs. They spoke of having to adapt to continual change, while needing to maintain order and consistency.

One of my research participants compared the concept of leadership and management to static and dynamic processes.

> *Management is the static side of the business. It is about ticking your boxes, the budget, and allocating resources. The dynamic part is the leadership part. You can't just be one or the other. You have to be out there and visible and working with your team. That is how you gain buy-in. I can sit here in this office all day long and not see anybody and I would never know their names, and they would never approach me to provide me with feedback. How can I make informed decisions if all I do is sit in my office?*

It was through the interviews and field observations that I began to develop a deeper understanding of the difference between management and leadership. But I still wondered how someone learns to become a manager and a leader. Many of the people I have spoken with throughout my career believe that leadership is an innate ability that you either have or don't, whereas being a manager is a skill that can be learned. In fact, some of the managers I interviewed in my research study held the same belief. When I asked them why they decided to become a manager, many of them said they had a mentor who saw something in them, a leadership quality that others in the organization did not possess. As a result, the mentor selected them for training for a formal leadership (i.e., managerial) position.

What surprised me was when I asked the question of how they acquired the skills required to be a manager, the process of learning to become a manager and a leader were very similar. In fact, they were not born with any special talent. They learned how to be a leader in the same way they learned to be a manager. They learned through moments of self-reflection, trial and error, asking lots of questions, and most importantly, developing relationships with others (e.g., supervisors, mentors, peers, and direct reports) who gave them honest and critical feedback on their performance.

Another popular method was observing and learning from other senior managers in their organization. Some managers they admired and others they did not. In other words, they learned what to do and what NOT to do. Through those observations they learned how best to engage their people through inspiration, not manipulation. Given these learning experiences, why do some people still hold the belief that leadership is an inherent ability? What are some of the consequences of holding onto that belief?

What if the person who holds that belief is the senior executive of an organization?

One of my colleagues, whom I will call him Tim, shared a story with me about hand selecting someone to develop due to what he perceived as innate leadership ability. Unfortunately, the person Tim hand-picked had no desire to move into a managerial position. But that did not stop my colleague from trying. Guess what happened? If you said Tim's efforts paid off, you would be wrong. Eventually, Tim gave up in frustration.

You see, Tim was following in the footsteps of his mentor who took the same approach with him. His mentor saw something in Tim that he believed was an innate leadership ability. Tim was repeating the cycle of what is called *traditional mentorship*, which is when someone, usually high up in the organization, grooms someone they select to develop. In contrast, *modern mentoring* is more inclusive because it is not based on a belief that leadership is something you are born with.

When you are a C-suite leader and you hand select people to mentor, you risk excluding a large population of your workforce from being developed, most commonly women. Around the world, there are few women in leadership positions in politics, on boards, and in organizations.[6] Having access to mentors, who are conducive to developing meaningful relationships with others at work, is a critical element in developing managerial and leadership ability. It is no surprise that strong leaders are able to develop strong and positive relationships in the workplace, which correlates positively with employee engagement and productivity.

Expansive workplace environments are collaborative and promote trust and inclusion through authentic interactions with others. Restrictive workplace environments are characterized by segregated working groups that are non-collaborative and exclude groups of employees from participating in certain activities, such as mentorship.[7] According to the Global Gender Gap Index, "the most challenging gender gaps to close are the economic and political empowerment dimensions, which will take 201 and 107 years to close respectively."[8] Yikes! That sounds pretty grim. Out of 149 countries assessed, there were just 17 that have women as heads of state, while only 18% of ministers are women. Likewise, where the data was available, it was found that 34% of managerial positions are held by women. That is why I devoted the last chapter to women in leadership, to bring to light the unique challenges we experience as we progress through our careers.

At the heart of manager and leadership development is working with other people and partnering with people whose skills and strengths are different than yours. An expansive workplace environment is inclusive, promoting and providing developmental opportunities, such as mentoring, for everyone.

You may be asking yourself why you should invest your time in others you have not personally selected. What's in it for me? What will the return be on that investment? According to Gallop, organizations face three rapid changes:

- radically shifting client and stakeholder demands
- rapid technological advancements
- new demands emerging from the next generation of employees.

If organizations do not have the ability to be nimble and adapt rapidly to such changes, they risk either losing out to their competitors or going out of business.[9] The quality of an organization's managers can be the lynchpin to agility and organizational success.

Therefore, the way an organization selects, promotes, and develops their managers can have reverberating implications for its long-term success. For instance, a common practice for organizations is to promote people into temporary managerial positions to fill a short-term vacancy (i.e., backfill for someone on holiday or a long-term leave). What the research has shown is that filling short-term vacancies is usually an ad hoc process that involves a senior manager or mentor guiding a person he or she believes would be a good replacement.[10] The experiential learning gained from short-term acting positions can assist an individual to gain the knowledge and confidence required to seek out other opportunities and take risks. It also acts as an instrument for individual enlightenment and organizational learning. It can improve someone's ability to respond to changing environmental demands. It can also increase morale since there are opportunities to be promoted from within.[11]

The number of women in the workforce between the ages of 25 and 54 has been increasing steadily.[12] In 2015, six million women participated in the labour market compared to 3.3 million in 1983. Women's experiences and access to leadership positions tend to differ from men's, having been shaped to a greater extent by their caregiving roles and their employers' beliefs about these roles.[13] It is important to consider the representation of women in formal leadership positions. Limited access to informal networks, influential colleagues, and mentors can create a barrier to upward mobility within an organization.

There are various theories as to why women are less likely to occupy leadership roles. One such theory is the "confidence gap," which states women have lower self-esteem than men and as a result they avoid promoting themselves unless they are 100% sure they can do the job, whereas men typically will jump right in believing they will succeed.[14] But there is also research that demonstrates women feel just as confident in their abilities and leadership skills as their male counterparts.[15]

Regardless of whether the confidence-gap theory holds water or not, it does place pressure on women to change versus asking organizations to shoulder some of the responsibility to ensure they are creating equitable workplace practices for development and promotion. Personally, I think the confidence-gap theory is bullshit. It can give organizations an excuse to place all the responsibility on women. As I mentioned above, filling short-term vacancies is usually an ad hoc process that involves a senior manager or mentor selecting someone they know and support. The on-the-job learning gained from temporary positions can increase someone's knowledge and *confidence*, which is advantageous in general but especially when a permanent position becomes available. Confidence comes from getting feedback and support from others in the workplace. Individuals learn through purposeful interaction in social settings.[16] Managerial learning is complex and typically involves simultaneous use of different types of knowledge and skills.[17]

Research shows that most learning is not just what an individual does on their own. It is also an integral part of normal work practices.[18] Support from colleagues can make it easier for you to take on challenges at work. C-suite leaders need to create equitable and inclusive strategies that embrace the ideas and outlooks of women; after all, half of humanity is female.

I heard Sir Ken Robinson give a TED talk regarding education in the United States, which I found inspiring.[19] "The real role of a leader is not command and control, but climate control. Creating the right climate of possibility." Investing in workplace learning strategies should not be seen as a cost or too time-consuming. It is an investment in our organization and our people. If the conditions in the workplace change to support learning, the relationships between managers and their team members will grow. People will be creative and take risks, which will lead to inspiring, engaging, and supportive workplaces.

Time to Reflect:
1. **How does your organization identify and select people for promotion?**
2. **Who typically gets invited to participate in social and informal networking activities (e.g., sports tournaments, lunches, etc.) and/or mentoring opportunities?**
3. **Explain the rationale for that practice and how it may influence opportunities for advancement.**

PART 1

The Undiscovered Learning Environment

1

MIND THE GAP

My PhD research focused on how managers learn partly because I didn't want other managers to struggle the way I did early in my career. I began scanning the research and to my surprise, there was little out there about how organizations develop their managers and the impact it has on their performance.[20] This gap is surprising given how much money organizations spend on training. The 2019 Training Industry Report notes that U.S. training expenditures totaled $83 billion.[21]

Anyone who has been a manager knows that we have to function within a certain amount of ambiguity. We deal with complex problems on a regular basis. Therefore, the workplace as a fruitful learning environment should be a key focus of all managerial development. But many organizations concentrate mainly on training opportunities. Organizations need to create a climate for managers where continual learning is not only supported but is embedded in workplace culture. This will enable managers to foster a learning environment for their teams. But what is the difference between training and workplace learning? What is the difference?

Training can be defined as a structured learning event, such as on-site courses, e-learning, and university courses where a credit is usually awarded. Conferences could also fit under this category. At times I have seen e-learning categorized as workplace learning, but I disagree. If the course is structured, has learning outcomes with a clear beginning, middle, and end, then it is training. The reason e-learning, conferences, and courses are defined as training is that they don't occur naturally as a part of everyday work.

In contrast to training is workplace learning, which is unstructured, opportunistic, and usually occurs spontaneously. I also use the term informal learning as a synonym to workplace learning, since the majority of informal learning occurs ad hoc. Informal learning can also occur during conferences, such as during conversations at networking events that provide people with opportunities to learn from others.

Workplace learning can occur on a continuum from structured to less structured. For example, coaching and mentoring moments could be categorized under structured workplace learning. Time is usually set aside and there is an intended outcome, such as when you are being mentored for career advancement. But coaching and mentoring can also occur spontaneously, as when a manager seeks advice from a trusted colleague before engaging in a difficult conversation with a team member.

Ideally, learning should lead to acquiring new knowledge in addition to modifying behaviour. If the knowledge we gain doesn't influence our performance, can it be considered learning? I'd say no. Learning takes a lot of time and practice and it is not always easy. It takes a certain amount of self-awareness to accept what you do not know and the courage to try new things and receive feedback from others. Many of my research participants admitted they were challenged in transferring what they learned from a course to their everyday work practice. So, the question still begs. Why don't organizations invest more in workplace learning? Many organizations invest in continual improvement processes in an effort to gain an edge over their competitors. When learning is purposefully embedded in everyday work, it can increase agility and resiliency within individuals. The more agile and resilient people are, the more they will be willing to try new things and embrace change. The alternative is repeating old behaviours and implementing archaic procedures that are doomed to fail. Continual improvement requires continual learning. How can an organization improve without learning something new? For new knowledge to be leveraged and put to good use, it cannot focus only on the acquisition of information. It has to support changes in performance.[22]

I remember when my organization integrated a new IT system that was supposed to create efficiencies that would allow us to focus our attention on more critical tasks. Training manuals were developed, and individuals were selected and trained to become lead trainers. When the system was implemented after a significant training period, it did not have the outcome our C-suite leaders anticipated. It actually doubled everyone's workload. We began to implement new manual processes, because people had no faith in the new system. In fact, there were times when the data we inputted was not retrievable. Some of it was human error and some of it was glitches in the system, highlighting the importance of continuous improvement processes that integrate feedback loops between users and system developers. If managers were built into the continuous improvement process, many of the issues would have been identified early on and fixed.

Unfortunately, many of the managers had not received training and were challenged in using the system properly. In fact, some managers led the charge in complaints and encouraged their team to sidestep the system. Now imagine a different scenario where managers were given the knowledge, tools, and skills to use the system properly. Managers could easily have been empowered as change agents to embed use of the system in everyday work practices and habits, leading to the successful implementation of a multi-million-dollar IT system. Instead, work had to be redone, off-setting any cost savings the system was intended to generate.

But how can a manager implement improvements in systems and processes successfully if she is not able to conduct some of the most basic duties of a manager? Remember, most managers learn through trial and error with little support for learning how to do the job. Take the task of delegation, for instance. It is not uncommon for a manager, especially new managers, to have a difficult time delegating tasks, causing them to be overburdened with responsibilities. But managers pay a high price when they don't learn how to delegate. It can result in being overworked and conducting many tasks superficially. The resulting chaotic work environment makes the job very complex and challenging.[23] Typically, managers are expected to figure out how to do the job with very little to no guidance, which can have embarrassing initial consequences.

The workplace is changing rapidly and as a result, managers need to evolve their supervisory methods. Think about your workplace and the type of work you do. Is it character-ized by discrete individualized tasks conducted in isolation? Or is it better described as project-based work that depends on collaboration?[24] To be more successful in project-based work, employees need to make decisions with autonomy and support from their managers. That means managers must be able to develop trusting relationships with their team so they can delegate.

Nevertheless, many organizations still view work and learning as separate categories that never overlap. Work is about achieving deliverables and results. Learning is about education. Training is also seen as something that might be necessary at the beginning of a new job, but not as critical as you advance into formal leadership positions. Just because an individual may have mastered the skills required as a technical worker it does not mean she is capable of manag-ing a team of her peers with little support or guidance. For new and existing managers alike, the philosophy of "learn as you go" becomes increasingly difficult to tolerate.

The type of culture created within an organization can limit the amount of learning that can occur in the work-place. Command-and-control style management inhib-its individuals. A culture of blame where leaders punish mistakes fosters distrust. Workplace relationships that do not include trust or tolerance are a barrier to learning.[25] Managers must balance the immediate demands of the or-ganization against the needs of their employees. A manager needs to support and inspire her employees to improve and sustain employee engagement, in addition to modeling the company's values.

Managers control how much autonomy their employ-ees have and how demanding their workload is. Managerial expertise can support organizational strategies, but many organizations still view managers' development as something that occurs naturally. Organizations should invest in creating dynamic, flexible, and inclusive workplaces. They should focus on the best ways to support workplace learning that considers the vibrant and ambiguous environment that is the manager's typical domain.

Time to Reflect:
1. **Think about a time, past or present, when your company implemented a new system that was supposed to create efficiencies in everyone's work.**
   a. **How did the company support employees in learning how to use the new system?**
   b. **What were the results?**

2

THE NATURE OF WORKPLACE LEARNING

Globalization is affecting the way organizations share knowledge and compete in today's global market economy. Client and stakeholder interests are in contention. The demographics of the labour market are in flux. Managers are becoming accustomed to constant changes in the organization and to responding to unique situations with limited time to think.[26] In such volatile working contexts, skills and competencies need continual development. Methods for exploring workplace learning have to expand to include a range of processes and systems that enhance managerial performance.

As I've noted above, most of managerial learning does not come from training opportunities but is embedded in normal work practice. Support from colleagues and confidence in one's abilities to take on challenging tasks impact learning in the workplace. These factors in turn influence how well managers value their contributions to the organization and the quality of their relationships at work.

The term workplace learning has been used increasingly in the training industry over the last few years for several reasons. Workplace learning is a contrast to training because it delivers a larger context where learning can happen. Learning from others in the workplace introduces a wider diversity of settings than training can offer. Research on workplace learning by professionals, technicians, and managers has revealed that learning in the workplace is mainly informal and involves observing others, mentoring, and learning from personal experiences.[27] Organizations can profit from workplace learning by discussing how it can be enhanced to enable managers to learn more efficiently in their day-to-day work. Although some organizations do offer workplace learning mechanisms such as coaching and mentoring, there is an array of other learning methods to consider as well.

As the old adage goes, experience is the best teacher. Learning comes from actively engaging with others and the world. It's learning by doing.[28] Of course, not all experience lends itself to learning. In fact, some experience can impede learning. But what constitutes experiential learning? Many 20th century scholars gave experience a central role in their theories on learning. They believed that learning is a continuous process grounded in experience and tested during experimentation. People learn using different strategies shaped by their environment. The ability to learn is not the result of a personality trait.

An experience may never become a learning moment if learning is not the intended outcome. Individuals are involved in a continuous flow of experience throughout their lives. Experiences become meaningful and contribute to learning when they are given attention and reflected upon. By simply paying attention to an experience it brings that experience into conscious thought so that it can be comprehended and acted upon rather than remaining on an unconscious level.[29]

A manager's learning is best shaped when she has a considerable amount of self-awareness regarding her strengths, limits, self-worth, and capability. Donald A. Schön in his book *The Reflective Practitioner* refers to this as *reflection-in-action*.[30] It occurs when something in the environment makes you aware of something out of the ordinary that requires special attention. Reflection is conscious—it causes people to question their assumptions of what they have always known to be true, which Schön refers to as *knowing-in-action*. If we always defer to completing an assignment based on "the way it has always been done," we will never take a risk and try something different. The wonderful thing about reflection is that it gives rise to on-the-spot experimentation. For instance, a manager may approach a task differently if she had time to reflect on what worked well and what didn't. The importance of reflection-in-action is the importance of improving performance.

Ideally, all action in the workplace should be based on learning that comes from reflection. More importantly, managers must take action based on what they believe is true while also considering other people's point of view, which can sway a manager's course of action. Throughout the day a manager has to integrate her thoughts with her feelings, which influence what she says and does. The more self-aware a manager is, the more skilled she will be at finding solutions to challenging problems.

If a manager's on-the-job learning constitutes mostly "sink or swim" occurrences, he will never have time to reflect-in-action on what worked and what didn't. This may result in choosing a certain course of action that has worked in the past (knowing-in-action), because there is little time to search for an alternative solution that may be better. This is common in fast-paced workplaces where people become overworked and overwhelmed.

A distinguishing feature of employees who have accumulated a massive amount of knowledge through experience is not how much they know but how their knowledge is organized for rapid, efficient, and effective use.[31] This knowledge gradually becomes part of people's habits, procedures, decision-making, and ways of thinking. It is influenced by social processes on the conscious and semi-conscious level, such as norms, values, perspectives, and interpretations of events.

One risk that workplace learning can pose is the creation of a personal bias. Unusual and noticeable occurrences tend to be remembered more than everyday behaviour, which can be problematic. For example, a manager is more likely to remember and reflect on a direct report's behaviour that is atypical than typical. Biases can influence a manager's workplace learning and affect his judgment, confidence, decision-making, and relationship-building. A way to mitigate bias is to become aware of assumptions and collect more evidence to control prejudice. As I have mentioned before, self-awareness is critical to checking biases, which can lead to growth.

Time to Reflect:
1. How does learning occur in your workplace?
2. What are some ways learning can be supported within your work context?
3. What are some ways you can make time in your workday to engage in self-reflection?

3

WHY TRAINING FAILS

Learning cannot exist independent of the social context. My research is based on this assumption; in qualitative research, we call this a philosophical paradigm. This assumption or paradigm is critical to my argument about why training fails in developing confident and capable managers. A lot of research into workplace learning is based on socio-cultural workplace learning theories. Stay with me here—I promise it will begin to sound interesting! Socio-cultural workplace learning theories are based on the belief that individuals make sense of their world through interaction with others and their social context.[32]

Knowledge is essentially developed, communicated, and interpreted within a social context. Furthermore, I cannot emphasize enough the importance of culture in behaviour and how we acquire knowledge. Without culture, humans cannot function. Humans depend on culture to direct and influence their behaviour and organize their experiences. All reality is constructed through social life and therefore, learning cannot exist independent of the social context. Or in this case, the workplace context. Workplace learning is significantly shaped by social, organizational, and cultural factors.[33]

The perspective of workplace learning opposes earlier generations of learning theories, which see learning as a product that can exist independently of the individual learner and from the context in which it is learned. If you believe this theory, then you would assume learners can easily transfer knowledge and skills from training to diverse situations and contexts, because learning is independent of context. Think of behaviourist learning theories. Remember Pavlov's dog and classical conditioning?[i] Behaviourist learning theories assume individuals are passive learners who start off as a clean slate, a *tabula rasa*. According to these theories, behaviour is shaped by positive or negative reinforcement.

Eventually, a new theory, called cognitivism, came along and challenged behaviourism. Cognitivism focused on thoughts and ideas as an important phenomenon in learning. But when cognitive scientists attempted to implement their theories in the classroom, they ran into a few problems. They discovered that students could not always generalize their newly acquired knowledge to different contexts. It was not as simple as retrieving knowledge from memory and applying it to a new situation. People's cognitive processes, such as thinking, are constructed in conjunction with aspects of our culture, like values and norms.[34]

Socio-cultural workplace theories eventually came along and offered alternative ways of thinking about how individuals learn by rejecting the idea that learning is independent of the workplace context. They also challenged the

---

i   Classical conditioning refers to a learning phenomenon in which a stimulus (e.g., dog food) is paired with a neutral stimulus (e.g., a bell) to cause a biological reaction (e.g., every time the bell rings, the dog drools).

idea that learning is either individual or social manifestation. Instead they argue learning can be individual, social, or both. Learning is an on-going process of participation in a variety of activities.

What does all of this mean for managerial learning? Managers transfer the knowledge they gain from training to the workplace in complex ways. For newly acquired knowledge to be transferred and used in the workplace, further learning and practice must occur so it can be ready for use in a range of work contexts.[35]

Karen Evans and Helen Rainbird, researchers in workplace learning, have used the analogy of the iceberg to explain this principle. Knowledge gained from training is at the "tip" of the iceberg, which lies just above the surface of the water. The underlying knowledge associated with workplace processes is represented by the large mass of ice below the water's surface and is largely invisible. Much of this learning is "tacit" or as mentioned before, unconscious to the individual; it gets minimal support and its very existence is often denied.[36]

Michael Eraut, whose research into informal learning influenced my research, states that two phenomena occur in the transfer of learning. First, for knowledge to be used in a particular situation it has to be transformed in a manner that fits the new situation. This process involves analysis and examination of a situation until a potential course of action seems appropriate. Second, in most situations several types of knowledge have to be combined for problem-solving to occur. But the ways the knowledge is used remains mostly tacit. This led Eraut to the important conclusion that the transfer of knowledge from training to workplace settings is much more complex than commonly thought. Transfer of learning from training to the workplace involves five inter-related stages:

1. Retrieving knowledge acquired from training (i.e., extracting it from our memory).
2. Understanding the new situation, which involves informal learning.
3. Identifying which knowledge and skills are relevant.
4. Transforming them to fit the new situation.
5. Integrating them into our existing knowledge and skills to think/act/communicate in the new situation.[37]

Think about your workplace. Are there mechanisms in place to support the five transfer of learning stages when someone returns from training? The truth is, most workplaces give some attention to stage three, but take stage two for granted. Many organizations assume that knowledge gained from training is ready-to-wear. So, they don't provide support mechanisms to encourage the transfer of learning to the workplace context.

Although I am certain managers gain knowledge from training, the challenge is to transfer that knowledge to the workplace context. Processes such as observing others, mentoring, and reflecting can support the transfer of learning. Self-reflection can also support taking learning back to the workplace. When time is given for reflection, a manager will be in a better position to determine how the knowledge he gained from a course applies to his work.

Consider workplace learning occurring on a continuum of conscious to unconscious levels and that self-reflection plays a vital role in the levels of learning awareness. More often than not, when managers engage in everyday work, any learning that may occur goes unnoticed. Learning can become an unintended and unnoticed consequence. A challenge for managers is to become more aware of what they are learning when they are engaged in working with others and mastering challenging tasks. Mike Myatt wrote an article in *Forbes* where he stated that "training is often a rote, one directional, one dimensional, one size fits all, authoritarian process that imposes static, outdated information on people. The majority of training takes place within a monologue (lecture/presentation) rather than a dialogue." Managerial learning is nuanced, contextual, and collaborative, not rote; this is one of the reasons why training fails.[38]

So much of what managers learn through day-to-day work goes undetected (the case with most workplace learning). Think about your workday. How often do you stop and notice all the things you are learning and picking up from others? What a manager learns in the workplace will most likely go undetected unless an unusual circumstance or a trigger brings the incident into consciousness. Workplace learning events are not likely to be interpreted as learning unless we can hone in on the experience in a particular way.

All of this makes researching workplace learning a huge challenge. One way I mitigated the challenge was to use case study research. Case study enabled me to examine managers' learning in the actual workplace context. It gave me the ability to focus on the social and contextual world of my research participants as well as their experiential knowledge. Through interviews and workplace observations, I was able to uncover what managers learn in the workplace, how they learn in the workplace, and the workplace factors that enable or impede learning.

I am very excited to share what I discovered through my PhD research. One of the biggest discoveries I made over the course of my professional and academic career is that managerial development, which occurs primarily in the workplace, is dependent on the relationships and supports a manager receives. A manager's learning is enhanced through his and her relationships. It is through these relationships that managers can seek different perspectives that can lead to modifying previously held beliefs and assumptions. I hope what my readers take away is a new perspective on managerial learning and development.

Time to Reflect:
1. **How did you learn to do your job?**
   a. **How much came from training versus workplace learning?**
2. **What are some mechanisms in your workplace that support the transfer of learning?**

PART 2

The What and How of Managerial
Development

4

WHAT MANAGERS LEARN THROUGH EVERYDAY WORK

My first research question focused on what managers actually learn in the workplace. What competencies do they have to master to become confident in their role? As I progressed through my data analysis there were two themes that emerged: leadership and manager competencies. One of my research participants, Eric, said, "I should mention I never did say leadership. I guess I take it for granted; being in the role it is essentially all leadership. I think it is very important…to lead to guide people, it starts before you become an actual supervisor…it comes with confidence." The managers in my study made the distinction between leadership and management. As I mentioned earlier, I used to believe being a manager is the same thing as being a leader. But over the course of my research, I started to understand that they are not the same thing and both competencies are required for a manager to be successful.

Managers are faced with multiple dilemmas. For instance, managers in the study expressed the importance of considering the larger system they worked within while considering the needs of their organization and team members. They spoke of having to be adaptable to continuous change, while needing to maintain order and consistency. Managers have to be able to think about achieving and monitoring results, while inspiring and motivating employees to be committed to their work and the organization.

Some of my research participants discussed how some of their leadership and manager competencies were acquired through training, but a lot of it was learned in the workplace by observing others, solving complex problems, and collaborating with others. For managers to be able to balance the divergent needs of their organizations, they need to be skilled leaders and managers. For a full list of themes and categories that fall under each of my research questions, refer to Appendix A. (You may find it useful to tear it out and use it as a guide for reading chapters 4, 5, and 6.)

Leadership Competencies

There were certain behaviours my research participants shared that seemed to fit together naturally under four separate categories. Once I began to group the behaviours together, I had an epiphany. It was almost as if the data reached out and slapped me across the face. The four categories were self-awareness, self-management, social awareness, and relationship management, in essence, the four domains of emotional intelligence (EI). Goleman, Boyatzis, and McKee wrote a book titled *Primal Leadership,*[39] from which I drew inspiration to support the results of my data. In research, theories can become more credible and trustworthy if the phenomenon you uncover has been researched by other scholars, and in this case it was.

Before breaking down each category, it is important to note that the first two categories determine how well a manager can regulate her emotions, while the last two categories determine how well a manager can recognize and manage the emotions of others. I mention this because a role of a manager is to inspire others to act and to work towards the successful completion of assignments. That would be hard to do if you were not able to master conflict, which is a common and natural part of every work environment.

In the next few chapters, I will share direct quotes from the managers in my study to illustrate the concepts more vividly. I have used pseudonyms to protect their names.

Self-Awareness

Managers expressed the importance of being aware of their strengths and limitations so they could continually develop and grow. "When I get to this situation where I run out of knowledge, I have to reboot or re-educate myself to new things. My competencies haven't changed a lot, but I have to focus on improving them," noted Daniel.

Curtis reiterated the importance of accurate self-assessment.

> *You have to be willing to accept that you don't know everything, rely on the people that know more than you. You have to be open, willing to change and accept change, know the things you can't control like political influence and budgets, and you have to be positive. I think that is a conscious decision every day. You have to be what you want everyone else to be. Whether you want to be that [on that] day or not.*

Boyatzis and McKee have referred to this as *resonant leadership*.[40] Resonant leaders work hard to develop not only their own EI, but that of others around them. Resonant leaders can integrate organizational priorities with the needs of their staff to achieve positive results. Having strong EI is not the only requirement to be an effective manager. A manager also requires management competencies such as the ability to oversee processes and implement strategies to deal with the challenges their organizations face, which I will get into in more detail in the next section. What makes a manager effective is not what he knows but how he uses his knowledge. Emotions and cognitive processes are intricately linked and can drive a manager's behaviour, especially during times of high stress.

Another critical aspect of self-awareness is confidence, as eloquently expressed by Aaron.

I still don't feel as comfortable as a new director. As a manager I have my assistants, my supervisors...as a director you have more people coming to you for information. It's a different feeling; it is a matter of becoming more comfortable in myself and becoming more comfortable, and the more I do it the better I will get at it. Practice and repetition—that is how I learn best.

Learning at work involves being proactive in seeking learning opportunities, which requires confidence. Taking on new challenges and confidence are interrelated in the sense that confidence is required to seek out new learning opportunities, but confidence is developed when managers meet challenges successfully. The confidence to take on new challenges depends on the extent to which managers feel supported by their colleagues. As a manager moves up the ranks to higher levels of management, support can begin to dwindle, as Eric clearly articulated.

There are fewer people that you can turn to for help as you climb the ranks. More eyes turn to you...it is a sheer numbers game. There are more employees than managers; it is a pyramid...so the people you look up to...are so many fewer each step up.

This feeling of isolation has been referred to as *power stress* by Boyatzis and McKee. Power stress can occur when a manager has to make a decision with ambiguous or little information in conjunction with fewer people to rely on for support. Therefore, managers need to be able to manage their own stress to sustain success over the length of their career. Being a manager can be exciting, but it can also be very stressful, which can lead to burnout. If managers are not self-aware enough to know when they are feeling burnt out, they may become trapped in a cycle of sacrifice that leads to lower emotional intelligence. Therefore, managers have to be able to implement self-care strategies to be able to renew their energy reserves.

During one of our interviews, Nick commented that he gets a lot of satisfaction from leading a team of people, but it does come with its challenges. For instance, he talked about the challenges of balancing the needs of the organization (reduce costs and ensure policies are being followed) with the needs of his staff (approve training requests and annual leave). Nick's method of combating power stress was to engage in activities outside of his work environment (e.g., running marathons and participating in recreational sports teams). This was a common strategy for many of my research participants, which leads me to the next category.

Self-Management

From self-awareness comes self-management, which involves being transparent and openly admitting to mistakes and faults, as articulated by Bobby.

> *I know this is one of the...values, accountability. Staff have to know that you are going to be accountable for your decisions and accountability is absolutely a two-way street. If I'm not willing to accept accountability and responsibility for my actions, what does that say to the staff? And also, conversely, if I make a mistake, I let staff know that I made a mistake. I don't see enough supervisors and managers doing that.*

Self-management also includes the ability to exert self-control in challenging situations or high stress situations. As Rina noted, "You have to manage yourself. That is your integrity, ethics, your personal role-modeling, and your own self-learning. You can't always rely on courses to help you out. You have to self-learn."

Phillip talked about the importance of being able to manage disturbing emotions and impulses, which he referred to as "triggers." One of my other research participants, Emily, also expressed the importance of being able to stay calm in a crisis:

> *There were multiple issues that happened in the span of a few hours. Literally every two seconds I was getting*

called because there was another crisis happening. Everyone saw me be hands-on, giving direction. I wasn't sure what I was doing but I was making decisions. I thought, I know what I know, so just go with it. That was the craziest thing that ever happened to me in my career. I asked for feedback afterwards. People went to my boss and said I did really good. It started a good bond with my team.

Managers who can exhibit self-control and manage their emotions have a sense of efficacy and take initiative. They take control of the situation and seize opportunities instead of waiting for them to happen. This was articulated by Phillip when he explained why he wanted to become a manager.

I would take on any opportunity. I was a trainer, I was part of the mentoring program for a while, all the things I could gather and learn from, led to being able to mentor and coach others. It only made sense to continue in a managerial role. I felt like I experienced everything I could as a frontline employee.

Initiative also involves challenging the process. In Kouzes and Posner's book, *The Leadership Challenge*,[41] they reveal that every single leadership case they collected involved challenging the status quo. None of the leaders they interviewed stated they achieved their personal best by keeping things the same. For example, managers are willing to step outside their comfort zone to grow and improve themselves, others, and the organization. As Curtis stated, "Now that I got comfortable in [my] role, I like that

I am in a position...that I can make real time changes, not just complain about it and not have the authority to actually do something about it." Jeff discussed the importance of being passionate about the work he did.

> *You have to be passionate with what you are doing, you have to believe in what you are doing. If this is just a paycheque, then you will be one of those slugs that do the bare minimum to get by. You will make sure you are following policy.*

In addition to having initiative and passion, managers also display other characteristics such as empathy and commitment. This brings me to the next category.

Social Awareness

The category of social awareness includes concepts such as empathy (e.g., understanding the emotions of others), organizational awareness (e.g., awareness of the guiding values and culture of the organization), and service (e.g., to others in the organization). Managers who demonstrate social awareness listen attentively and are able to grasp the other person's perspective. The managers in my research study expressed the importance of being able to blend managerial duties, such as performance management, with employee engagement strategies that included rapport building to develop trust and empathy between themselves and their employees. Greg described how he demonstrated empathy, encouraged delegation of tasks, organizational awareness, and service toward the people in his organization.

You still have to make sure that all of your staff are doing ok, [that] they have whatever is needed to assist them and I make suggestions to them, "Why don't you hand that off to somebody else." You need to care. [You make sure] your staff has the support they need to make decisions...I try to remember people's names or congratulations on the new baby...It is important to have those personal conversations, because I do care. It isn't a façade or pretending and any good supervisor needs to have that and a leader needs to be able to connect with the people they lead.

Greg's account of social awareness is also an example of relationship management, which is the final category I will discuss.

Relationship Management

Relationship management is about the ability to inspire others, influence others to act, resolve conflicts, build bonds, and develop others by fostering teamwork and collaboration. I call this the *heart* category, although in actuality EI is all about heart! As Phillip expressed so eloquently, "You want to empower your staff so they feel competent. You don't want to do their work...but you want to show them that you trust them." Managers cultivate people's abilities and show sincere interest in other people's well-being by taking time to provide feedback and guidance through mentoring and coaching opportunities. Rick expressed that very clearly in one of our interviews.

The most important thing for a manager is to be a good mentor. I had really good mentors in my career and I try to model myself after those mentors. I see other supervisors that are not as successful, and they do not have good mentors. They have a lot of knowledge, but they do not impart their knowledge....What also makes a good mentor is [they] lead by example.

Mentoring and coaching can give managers an opportunity to provide feedback to their staff. People can become exhausted, frustrated, disenchanted, and tempted to give up. Managers encourage through recognition and praise for a job well done so their staff can continue to be engaged in the workplace.

After I resigned from my position as a senior manager to launch my leadership consulting firm, Sinogap Solutions, I received a text from one of my team members. It read, "I really miss your energy, encouragement and positivity here." I always made a point to visit my team every morning to say hello with a big smile (even though there were days I was not in a good mood) to see how they were doing. I didn't realize it at the time, not until I got that text, that those simple moments went a long way in establishing trust with them. Recognizing contributions can be as simple as asking how your team is doing, sending a thank you e-mail for providing support on a project or recommending a strategy that worked. It is the small, consistently considerate things a manager does for her team that makes the biggest difference.

One other thing I would like to note about my previous team—Sinogap Solutions' logo consists of six sides. On my website it states that each side represents one of our six values. That is true, but each side represents something else as well. The last team I led as a senior manager was made up of six amazing women. Each side of my logo represents one of them. I did that so they could be a part of my team...forever. They will always be with me, in my mind and my heart.

Being a manager is about forming trusting relationships, which at times can encompass conflict. Being able to engage in conflict is actually a good way to gauge how much trust exists in a relationship. If you don't trust someone you may not be willing to express your feelings or thoughts, especially when they are in contrast to someone else's. Managers who can mitigate conflict are able to understand differing perspectives, acknowledge feelings, and redirect energy toward a common goal. Being able to manage conflict means you have to be willing to model accountability. Patrick Lencioni in his book, *The Advantage,* says this amazing thing: "When there is trust, conflict becomes nothing more but the pursuit of truth, an attempt to find the best possible answer."[42] Bobby's quote below illustrates the link between conflict, approachability, and inspiring others.

If I made a decision that has negatively affected a team member and I reflect afterwards that I could've done that differently with a more positive outcome, then I will go to that person and say I am sorry, I could've done this better. I want team members to say, "You know what? This guy is open to the idea that maybe he doesn't know everything." Some of the best things I learned have been from my staff, because they feel there is that level of respect and openness [and] they can come and tell me. I have always told my team that, if there is something they feel that I have done wrong, that has negatively affected them, and [they] don't understand why, they can come talk to me.

My research participants also talked about conducting "rounds" on a regular basis. Rounds give managers an opportunity to connect and touch base directly with their staff. In essence, that is what I was doing when I visited with my team every morning. Jacob, one of the managers in my study, explained how rounds provide opportunities to build relationships with staff, which in turn make it easier for staff to approach their supervisors. This was also illustrated by Zach during one of our interviews. "Good interpersonal skills…I think most people can be a manager but again, interpersonal skills come into your leadership. How people actually relate to you…trust is a big thing." Developing relationships was seen as critical to being an effective manager, because it contributes to an atmosphere of comradery, respect, and cooperation. As Jacob said, "The majority of the job is dealing with people…actually going to your staff. Making sure they know I am a resource for them."

Conducting rounds, in essence, is making yourself accessible to your team. In today's world, many managers have remote teams. Distance can present an added challenge to accessibility, but with today's technology there are a multitude of ways to stay connected. And if you don't have tech, then a good old-fashioned phone call will do the trick. Being accessible is critical to relationship-building. It allows managers to stay in touch with their teams, so they are aware of challenges and supports they need to be productive and successful. It also makes it easier for a manager to advocate for their team and shield them from decisions that may have negative impacts on their performance.

I used to work with a manager who was notorious for saying yes to every executive request that came across his desk, because he was afraid of the conflict that could arise by pushing back and saying no. This presented many challenges for his team. Eventually, they began to miss deadlines and submit work they weren't proud of. They expressed how their manager did not "have their back" and was only interested in reaping the rewards of their hard labour. Needless to say, the turnover in that team rivaled a department store's revolving door during a Black Friday sale.

Although every manager in my research study expressed the importance of possessing leadership competencies to lead successful teams, they also expressed the importance of overseeing systems, achieving results, and handling resources. This leads me to the second theme.

Manager Competencies
Under the theme of manager competencies, four categories emerged from my data analysis. They were:

1. Systems thinking
2. Controlling assets
3. Overseeing systems and processes
4. Achieving results

I began to understand the difference between leader and manager after hearing from managers in my research study. Although someone may hold the title of "manager," if she wants to be successful in balancing the divergent needs of the organization, she will need to be skilled in both leadership and manager competencies.

Systems Thinking
Systems thinking can be defined as recognizing links between how one's work contributes to the achievement of

organizational goals. This can include the anticipation of potential risks and impacts across interrelated areas when making decisions and considering opportunities for action. My research participants described systems thinking in an interesting way. To them it was the ability to think outside of the box by adapting and changing their line of thinking before making a decision or when seeking input by asking questions.

When I asked my participants if the nature of their competencies had changed since they acquired them, nearly all of them said the same thing. Competencies do not change, but the way you use them does. For instance, the ability to develop relationships and establish networks is important at any stage of a person's career. But knowing how to influence relationships and leverage networks is important when making decisions that will impact the team and organization. Emily expressed the importance of looking at the bigger picture and understanding the organization's vision, "Being exposed to the way the executive team thinks, you start buying into what they are trying to do. I can explain why things are done that way to my team. Definitely looking at the bigger picture and not just focused on what is in front of me."

Managers are responsible for systems thinking; it involves participation, empowerment, and commitment to the organization.[43] Systems thinking is about synthesis. It includes an integrated view of the organization. The managers in my study also conveyed the importance of thinking about the system during recruiting and succession planning, which leads me to the next category.

Controlling Assets
Controlling assets consists of common managerial duties such as scheduling staff, managing cover off when someone

calls in sick, and assigning work to team members. Rick, who worked in a 24-hour unionized operation, said that one of his biggest challenges was staffing. "Trying to fill a shift without using overtime, but inevitably it goes to overtime. Then there are staffing issues, like this one doesn't get along with this person or that person."

Controlling assets also consists of managing time and budget, and allocating resources such as equipment needed for the daily operation of the organization. "In terms of budget and resource allocation...in my previous position and that was someone sitting with me to teach me. I needed an admin to teach me the budget, the monthly reviews," said Curtis. Jeff expressed the importance of time management. "There are so many moving parts that you really need to know how to manage your time so that you don't get too focused on one issue so that other issues get neglected." In addition, Jeff conveyed that there are "so many things that go into managing this business. There are budget things and there are laws of how we manage employees. We have to learn outside the box." Tom illustrated the diverse responsibilities of a manager that are required during an "easygoing" day versus a "demanding" day.

You get one of two types of days. Some days are slower, so you are working on a lot of special projects and you have a lot of down time and you get out of the office and just go sit with your team, see what their issues are, have friendly conversations, what they are doing on days off, you know things like that. And then there are days where it is total chaos; I am doing incident reports from start till end of day. I'm hunting down

different individuals for different issues and mak-
ing sure that staff are getting the support they need,
things like that.

Understanding the organization's systems and processes helps a manager know how to manage assets efficiently. For example, knowledge of policies, legislation, and union agreements helps managers control staff resources. For many of the managers in my study, this understanding came primarily from learning informally in the workplace— learning from others (e.g., peers and direct reports) and having access to job aids (e.g., policy manuals and quick reference how-to guides). Although job aids were available to each manager, they did not always help them deal with difficult issues. During times of high stress, managers do not have the luxury of time to reflect and review policy manuals to guide their decision making. They become dependent on getting input and advice from others to know how to approach certain situations. This is another reason organizations need to shift their learning and development approaches toward workplace learning strategies and to rely less on training.

Overseeing Systems and Processes

Overseeing systems and processes involves knowing how to use all of an organization's infrastructure properly and efficiently, including data management software, reporting processes, employee management systems, finance systems, and union policies. The managers in my study commonly oversaw legal processes that governed their organizations' policies and practices. Bobby noted that, "As an assistant manager you would work in the manager's office so you should be learning their job and there is a large learning process there." For Eric, one of my participants, knowledge of legislation was critical for delegating and executing certain assignments. "You have to learn law, I have to have a fairly high knowledge base of law, of the legal system. A big job is to interpret the law when it comes to… legal cases…that have happened years and years ago that impacts the decisions we make."

Implementing processes also involves being able to apply assets in efficient and economical ways. I had the opportunity to observe such efficiency during one of my field observations. Managers had to use scheduling software to create good time management processes for booking 24-hour shift rotations to reduce overtime costs. To ensure the scheduling software was used properly, managers learned to use it through a training event (e.g., a course) so they could provide support and on-the-job training to other managers on their shift. I observed a manager requesting assistance from my participant, Zach, on how to use the software. I was impressed by how well Zach knew how to navigate the complex software while articulating the organizational benefits and the return on investment. This example of one person learning from another illustrates what managers learn and the informal processes that support their learning in the workplace.

Achieving and Monitoring Results

Progress should be assessed often and carefully to improve effectiveness and success in an organization. Managers must find ways to measure success so they can set new targets for performance each year. Participants in my study discussed the challenges to achieving and monitoring results. They also discussed being able to assess situations and decide on action to create a successful outcome. Participants in the study did not always have enough time when making decisions. Managers had to deal with complex, constantly changing situations and did not always have all the relevant information at their fingertips when making decisions. This was expressed by Rina when she accepted a new managerial position with a team she had never worked with before.

> *There was no course on how to manage [my team] and this office. So, I looked at my strengths and I said ok… just because I am a manager doesn't mean I know everything. I would go into [my team's] office and ask them why is something like this? That is pretty much how I learned, from the [people] around me and the manager from the north office. So, I learned from my staff, myself, and…my colleagues.*

Daniel also discussed making mistakes and being able to learn from them so that performance and practice could be continually improved. "Making mistakes, not wanting to make the same mistakes twice. I try not to steer the ship into the rocks—that would be bad for the organization. But I am ok with making mistakes. That is how I have to learn."

Being able to achieve results and monitor progress involved four interrelated stages of performance:

1. Assessing a situation, which managers sometimes did alone and other times with staff and other managers.
2. Deciding what action to take, which occurred in consultation with others.

3. Following a course of action, for instance giving directions and delegating duties.
4. Reflecting on how it went, for example, learning from what did and did not work.[44]

These processes did not always follow a simple sequence of assessment, decision, and then action. Eric, whose team provides meal service, gave an example of how the four stages occur in his work context.

Like meal service, a simple task. At [our other location] food came out hot and was served. Now we have the food delivered hours before it is served in a building that has so many people come and go, so...by the time we are serving food we have varying numbers for what we require. That is a big problem; we have been trying to solve it, but we can't expect our contract workers or the kitchen people to absorb all of that change, so we have to kind of meet them in the middle. It is one of those tasks that comes and lands on the manager's shoulders. Talk to people, find out what we can do, but you guys bring us the solution. That is one example of a large-scale problem-solving thing we have.

In these examples, making decisions that led to successful results was important for building confidence and skills in managers. Being able to learn at work was also critical for ongoing managerial development.

The ability to gain knowledge through the process of learning so that it influences performance is dependent on how emotionally intelligent a manager is. The four domains of emotional intelligence are not mutually exclusive to what managers learn, but are pertinent to their overall learning and development. An emotionally intelligent manager creates an environment where workplace learning is embraced. It promotes empathy and trust building. It supports forming relationships that foster the teamwork through which learning occurs.

Time to Reflect:
1. **Think about a leader you would categorize as emotionally intelligent. How do they develop trusting relationships with others?**
2. **In which ways have relationships supported and influenced your leadership and management development?**
3. **What are two actions you can take to develop trusting relationships with others?**

5

HOW MANAGERS LEARN THROUGH EVERYDAY WORK

I would like to take a moment to acknowledge Dr. Michael Eraut whose research into workplace learning has influenced my research and the creation of my theoretical framework, which forms the basis of the next two chapters. Dr. Eraut was a long-standing Professor of Education at the University of Sussex. He died in 2018, which I happened to find out as I was writing this chapter. Although I never had the opportunity to meet him (I sent an e-mail to him in 2017 acknowledging how much his work inspired me), I felt connected to his work and I admired him very much. The next two chapters are dedicated to him.

We have arrived at one of my favourite chapters. It examines how managers actually learn through everyday work. This chapter is important because it is where theory and practice join forces—where the rubber meets the road. I have read countless articles and watched dozens of webinars that attempt, with little success, to explain this phenomenon. As

I mentioned earlier, very little research has examined how managers learn through everyday work because much of our learning goes unnoticed. Therefore, we need to ask how we develop strategies to support workplace learning when the very nature of it is implicit. The next few pages will illuminate the various processes that contribute to a manager's workplace learning.

As I analyzed my data, four themes emerged:

1. Leadership competencies
2. Work processes
3. Learning processes within work
4. Learning activities

As I discussed earlier, I found that leadership competencies developed as a prominent theme under each of my three research questions—what are managers learning, how are they learning it, and what contextual workplace factors affect learning? Leadership competencies are important to supervisors and managers developing their skills in the workplace. Meaning, self-awareness, self-management, social awareness, and relationship management pertain to what managers learn and how they learn. Therefore, I will discuss leadership competencies within the context of work processes, learning processes, and finally learning activities. The figure below shows the relationship among the four themes.

The second, third, and fourth themes: work processes, learning processes within work, and learning activities were inspired by Michael Eraut's categorization of early career leaning with some minor adjustments.[45] What emerged from my data analysis is that learning processes are embedded within many work activities (e.g., problem-solving) and are not always explicit. Although learning occurred, the main objective was improving performance, not learning.

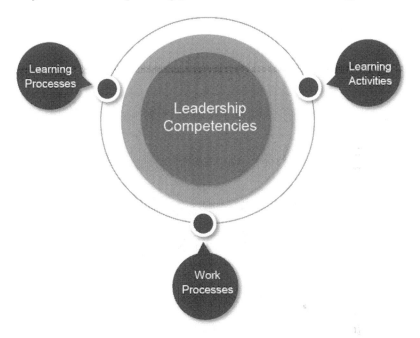

Whereas, learning *processes* are implicit and not always detectable, learning *activities* are overt. In other words, time is put aside to participate in a learning activity. Once again, the main objective of this type of learning is to improve performance, but the method of learning tends to be formal (e.g., courses) and occurs off the worksite.

Overall, participants' learning was gained primarily from participating in specific job-related activities in the workplace, consulting others by asking questions and requesting feedback, and solving day-to-day problems as they arose.

Work Processes: Learning is Implicit

Let's begin with work processes, which accounted for a high proportion of learning for participants in the study. Work processes included collaborating with others, gaining specific job-related experience in the workplace through acting positions, solving complex problems, consulting others, and the four stages of performance discussed in the previous chapter (i.e., assessing, deciding, action, and reflection). Leadership competencies, such as being self-aware and managing one's own and others' emotions, were explicitly expressed during the interviews and influenced how managers learned. For example, a self-aware manager is more likely to be honest about the gaps in her abilities and subsequently work with others (e.g., mentors) to request feedback and assistance in solving complex problems. Accordingly, being able to display qualities such as empathy, compassion, and genuine interest in working to develop self and others was intricately linked to all work processes.

> *A lot of people shy away from this role because it isn't easy, 130 staff per shift, different personalities. But that is the benefit of [being in an acting managerial] role. You know what you are getting into like staff conflict. Have to take control of the situation and guide it. You want to know you are doing the right thing. That kind of stuff is always in the back of your mind, if you are a good leader.* (Zach)

All of the participants in the study were exposed to acting positions. Acting positions are when an individual occupies a temporary managerial position to backfill for a manager who is away. Acting positions were directly related to how managers learned in the workplace. These types of assignments are opportunities for "trying out" a position before actually assuming a supervisory role. Every participant acted on an "as needed" basis in addition to longer-term opportunities—secondments—that lasted weeks or years. Acting positions and secondments also gave senior managers an opportunity to offer mentorship and to assess the competencies of the acting manager. Acting positions and secondments gave incumbents an advantage over other candidates when competing for a managerial position, due to the skills and confidence gained from the opportunity. This process became the organization's main method of identifying successors. Eric explained this concept in detail.

> *When I started acting as a manager, it was very outside of my comfort zone, it wasn't something I have done...I was training as a [file] manager. I would look at files, I would review, I would make notes, I would identify the things I was looking for, I would write down what I saw. And this was so the existing managers could review my work and check to see that I am interpreting things properly. That was for a three-month period where they reviewed my work till the point that they got comfortable with allowing me signing authority...so once that happened I relaxed a little, it was freeing for me cause it was a little vote of confidence that was important to me.*

Upper management recognized that many of their senior managers were going to retire, which would create a gap in the management workforce. Therefore, upper management developed a succession plan that gave employees an opportunity to take on various managerial positions over the course of a full year.

> *This year there was an informal competition for manager succession training. That was a year-long process that started. [Upper management] realized that a lot of the managers here are hitting that age where they are starting to think about retirement, so [upper management] started planning for succession. There were [several] of us that were selected...They wanted us... to experience everything, you should have knowledge of everything.* (Todd)

Working with others was also important for learning how to solve complex problems and working through the four stages of performance. By working closely with others, participants were able to observe, listen, and learn from more experienced officers (e.g., peers, subordinates, and managers). By observing others, participants learned new practices and perspectives, as expressed by Emily.

> *When I started acting, you have a fear. You double-check everything that you do, that is why I align myself with a mentor because they are the sounding board. I always second-guessed myself a year ago, now I am more confident 'cause I have a little bit more experience. I had a hard time sticking to a decision because I wondered if it was the right one. I learned through time, repetition, through feedback. Of course, it changes. You change by learning. The more you learn, the more skills you acquire.*

Working with others also included processes such as asking questions and receiving feedback, which were activities that presented opportunities for reflection and hence learning. This brings me to the next theme.

Learning Processes Within Work: Learning is Reactive

Learning processes within work were embedded within many of the work activities explained above (e.g., acting and seconded positions). What made the difference was the amount of conscious effort or awareness involved regarding the amount and quality of learning. Clearly, learning can occur spontaneously in response to a recent situation.

At times managers are unconsciously aware of their learning, while at other times learning occurs when time is set aside for reflection. For instance, asking questions and seeking feedback was done with the sole purpose of learning how to improve one's practice. Jacob, an experienced manager, discussed the importance of asking questions throughout his career so he could ensure he was learning and improving his skills. "I asked a lot of questions as a frontline employee watching supervisors, but it helped tie everything together because a lot of people are on their own. Some people want to learn. [When I was] a supervisor, I watched the manager and asked why you do this or that."

Some of the research participants approached senior managers and asked them how they would deal with hypothetical situations about complex problems. This was done with the purpose of being able to manage difficult situations, should they occur. As Bobby expressed it, "Asking hypotheticals. How would you deal with it? I do that on an on-going basis. I review incidents that I am not working on and I see how that was dealt with. And if there are any questions …then I go and ask somebody that is more in the know about that stuff."

Leadership competencies (e.g., self-awareness, self-management, and relationship management) were also critical in being able to ask for feedback. The managers in my study discussed the importance of receiving honest feedback and support from mentors they trusted. Zach noted, "Good leaders build good leaders who want to spend their time showing you how to do things, teaching you." Giving and receiving feedback were not just important, but vital for most learning processes. Consequently, learning in the workplace depended on the quality of relationships within one's workplace, as expressed by Emily.

Someone who is willing to impart their knowledge, teach and recognize opportunities to teach and does it in a manner that is not insulting. I see a lot of managers and supervisors who see things and just ignore it. A good mentor sees things and uses it as a teaching moment. For example, they will see something and say maybe this wasn't the best way to handle it. What also makes a good mentor is leading by example.

Job aid manuals and personal journals were also used with the express purpose of learning, as Curtis noted.

When I was a [frontline employee] trying to become a supervisor, I would look at the people that I thought were really good at the job and I had a notebook to write down what I thought was good...Just by me

*writing it down, it gave me the ability to say, ok, this is
the road I need to take.*

Many of the managers also expressed how participating in
special projects and committees contributed to their learning, such as "Committee work that helps with staff development," as Derek said. Managers in the study saw committee
work as an opportunity to learn more about the other parts
of the organization and to work with new people. As Rina
noted, "Taking on training was a new portfolio for me.
Walking around talking to the instructors, collecting data,
collecting information. Trying to learn not only the data and
information, but the politics."

Manager meetings were also an important activity. They
gave managers the ability to share information about what
is occurring in the entire department. Although learning
was at times reactive during manager meetings, they were
important for sharing personal and process knowledge.
Personal knowledge is what individuals bring to a situation
that enables them to think and perform. It includes knowledge of people, situations, and the "know-how" of skills and
practices. Process knowledge is about knowing how to conduct the processes embedded as part of normal work practices. It requires an individual to reflect on their knowledge
of people and situations. It was through manager meetings
that managers learned about various processes and systems so they could efficiently allocate resources and put assets to use.

Learning Activities: Learning is Deliberate
Learning activities are deliberate actions for the purpose of acquiring new knowledge and skills; time is put

aside for learning. This includes participating in formal training, which usually occurs off the worksite, such as university courses and conferences. The managers in the study discussed how education is a requirement to become a manager. "There is more focus on education if you want to become a manager. Now they require a university degree, which is what I am working on," said Emily.

There were occasions that the managers in my study attended learning activities such as conferences, but these opportunities were rare and experienced by less than a quarter of them. More common were courses and workshops offered through the organization (e.g., leadership courses). Managers reported that a small amount of their learning occurred through training. The majority of what and how they learned occurred through work and learning processes within the workplace.

I took some courses. I haven't taken a lot of courses and I don't have a lot of education behind me. How much of this did I draw from sitting in a classroom? I would say 10%. A little was classroom stuff. When it comes to performance and employee relations, like what you can and can't do, that is reading the [union] agreement and consulting with human resources. Like here, when I first came here, I couldn't tell you what the policies were...so I had to read and ask questions to learn. (Curtis)

Another manager explained how receiving a certificate from a course can look good on a resume, but doesn't help with learning how to do the job.

It [the certificate] can help on the resume [and] in an interview you can explain the transparent leader and the types of followers and it can sound really good, but it doesn't demonstrate [that I can do the job]...the courses helped me realize what I have always done. (Jacob)

Managers said they had challenges to being able to transfer knowledge gained from courses and workshops to the workplace. As Tom noted, "I took various leadership courses...but it didn't exactly help me with my job... sometimes it is difficult to find aspects of those courses that correlate to the job." One of the benefits of attending workshops and courses were "sidebar conversations that were informal but would become part of the formal part of the training," observed Greg. "Sidebar" conversations provided managers an opportunity to learn new things and generate ideas from people outside of their organization. This required leadership competencies on the part of the participants. Examples include seizing opportunities to strike up conversations and develop relationships with other people to foster a collaborative environment.

Managers' learning was gained primarily from within the workplace, but the quality and amount of learning that occurred depended on how well the workplace created opportunities for, or barriers to, learning. The final section of this chapter will present the results for the third research question: What contextual workplace factors affected informal learning by managers?

Time to Reflect:

1. What are some work processes you can leverage to support leadership and managerial development?

2. How would you structure those work processes to make learning explicit (e.g., you are consciously aware of what you are learning)?

6

WORKPLACE FACTORS THAT AFFECT MANAGERIAL LEARNING

As I discussed at the beginning of the chapter, all of the themes are interrelated concepts in the sense they are not isolated but work together to influence and inform what managers learn and how they learn it. This also includes contextual factors in the workplace that either create opportunities for, or barriers to, learning. Researchers have recognized the important role context plays in employee workplace learning.[46] Fuller and Unwin, workplace learning researchers, developed a theory to categorize barriers and opportunities to learning, which they term *expansive* and *restrictive*. Their research has focused on the interaction of organizational context, workplace learning, and individual learning, which align with the three themes that emerged from my data analysis:

1. Leadership competencies
2. Learning factors
3. Context factors

Each theme will be discussed based on its expansive or restrictive features within the workplace setting. The theme of leadership competencies will be discussed within the context of learning factors and context factors, which were inspired by Michael Eraut's informal workplace learning theory.[47] For a full list of expansive and restrictive features for learning and context factors, please refer to Appendix B and C.

Learning Factors

These learning factors influence an individual's ability to learn within a workplace context.

1. Confidence and commitment
2. Feedback and support
3. Challenge and value of work

Being open to taking on new challenges requires confidence. Confidence depends on the relationships at work and the type of feedback and support one receives from others (e.g., mentors). Managers in the study reported that feeling confident was important when seeking new learning opportunities and challenges, but their confidence depended on the extent to which they felt supported by their colleagues. "It comes down to self-development and career development. When I applied for a supervisor's job, I wanted a challenge and I enjoyed leading. In management roles, it is the ability to recognize people above you and beside you. You want to be surrounded by good people," said Zach. Bobby shared a story regarding a challenge he was hesitant to take on, but changed his mind after receiving support from one of his mentors.

The manager [told me] you can sit on the side lines and let other people that may not be as competent or capable as you advance, and you may be ok with that...However, if you are ok with that...what about the people that work with you. Are they ok with that... you have a lot of the skill sets that your coworkers don't have...you've told me that you care about them... how about working for them? So that convinced me [to become a supervisor]. I had reflection on that and that is what made me go forward and consequently that is what I said to other people to get them involved.

The quote from Bobby nicely captures an example of an expansive workplace environment that is conducive to employees developing confidence and commitment to their work. Examples of expansive learning factors include access to mentors who provide specific feedback to improve performance, forming bonds and positive relationships with people at work (e.g., relationship management), and offering support to staff after a crisis. Examples of restrictive learning factors are little to no access to mentors, employees disconnected and isolated from other peers, and no emotional support after a traumatic incident.

Context Factors

Context factors influence learning factors. For example, the amount of feedback and support a manager receives depends on the relationship she has with her mentor or peers. The categories under this theme are:

1. Encounters and relationships with others at work
2. Allocation and structuring of work

One important thing to mention is that mentorship occurs spontaneously through forming relationships and bonds in the workplace. Although there was a formal mentorship program offered through the organization, the majority of mentoring relationships came from an organic process. This was explained by Daniel.

> *During the start of my career I was learning with a group of people. We all got together and decided to [mentor each other] through interviews and competitions to try and get promoted. Over a 10-year period we have all been successful and have developed a great sense of teamwork amongst each other.*

Encounters and relationships with others at work are interrelated to the leadership competencies of social awareness and relationship management, competencies that enable managers to cultivate relationships within the workplace. Expansive workplace environments are collaborative environments that promote trust and inclusion through authentic interactions with others. Restrictive workplace environments are characterized by segregated working groups that are non-collaborative and exclude groups of employees from participating in certain activities.[48]

Managers in the study gave examples of both expansive and restrictive workplace environments. An example of an expansive work environment was given by Eric, "You pick up these competencies by working with other people, partnering up with more experienced people…They could be your superiors who have obviously been around longer and have climbed up that rank structure." Managers were seen as facilitators of workforce development within the organization who promoted collaboration among staff. An example of a restrictive work environment was given by Aaron, who expressed, "I never got feedback from my supervisors…[nowadays] a lot of people in acting roles… will personally come to me and ask me, 'what am I doing right and what I am doing wrong?' They want that feedback." This provides an example of how important it is to create expansive learning environments that include feedback loops so individuals can be aware of the gaps in their performance.

In addition to the important role relationships play in managerial development, allocating and structuring work is also critical. Allocating and structuring work deals with how time and workplace pressures influence a manager's ability to think and make decisions. The four stages of performance (i.e., assessing a situation, deciding what action to take, following a course of action, and reflection after the action) involve thinking about how to carry out these activities, which depends on the manger's ability and prior learning. At times, the situation allows for thoughtful analysis of the situation so that decision making is more deliberate, while in other circumstances the situation calls for a rapid decision.

Time is the variable that influences a manager's ability to think through situations. The more time a manager has to think, which occurs in slower-paced work environments, the easier it is to assess, think, and reflect before making a decision, as in reflection-in-action, as we discussed in chapter two. In other instances, such as dealing with brief, near-spontaneous events, which I characterize as *thinking on your feet,* snap decisions need to be made, as in knowing-in-action.

Slower-paced work environments are ideal and conducive to building confidence, especially with new managers or even seasoned managers joining a new organization. Therefore, the allocation and structure of work for a manager needs to be sufficiently challenging without being too overwhelming. Emily discussed how experience and time were needed to be successful as a manger.

> *You can't be rushed through. You need time in and you need knowledge of policies, procedures and operations, 'cause if you don't, you can't make proper decisions…You double-check everything that you do, that is why I align myself with a mentor cause they are the sounding board…now I am more confident 'cause I have a little bit more experience…I learned through time, repetition, through feedback.*

As mentioned above, on the opposing end of slower-paced environments are spontaneous occurrences that require an immediate response. Eric gave an example of this, "Emergency [situations] require a supervisor to be quick thinking and sound in [their] judgment." Managers have to make snap decisions and have confidence in those decisions. At times, this wasn't the case as expressed by Aaron.

> *There was an incident… I went up there. I am going to admit, I was new there, I was by myself and I did feel uncomfortable. I panicked, I ended up calling for all*

available staff to come there, which probably wasn't the smartest thing I did.

During those instances, it was crucial that a debrief followed to provide time to reflect and learn from mistakes.

I was the first person to admit that I didn't do it all right. It was one of the better [debriefs] we had because we discussed it and I think I gained back a lot of confidence having done that. And I never did that mistake again. It was a learning experience. It is humbling... admitting to your staff that you didn't handle things properly. We are always going to make mistakes; it is just the severity of the mistake and how you are going to control it. (Aaron)

Debriefs serve multiple functions, one of which is as a method of reflection on how to improve performance (e.g., what we learned from the incident and how we can approach it differently next time). Another important function of a debrief is to assess the emotional well-being of others (e.g., emotional intelligence). Incidents are stressful occurrences that pose a high amount of risk to employees. Through a debrief, a manager can display empathy and compassion for others who report to him or her. Debriefs provide a strong example of the dynamic relationship between what managers learn, how they learn, and contextual workplace factors that affect learning. Ultimately, effective decision-making relies on the manager's framing and understanding of the situation and her personal knowledge about the situation.

Time to Reflect:

1. In which ways have mentors supported your leadership and managerial development?
2. How has feedback influenced your performance?
3. How can workloads be structured in your workplace to support leadership and managerial performance?

7

PUTTING IT ALL TOGETHER

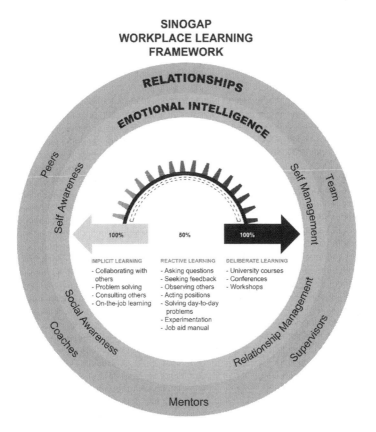

SINOGAP
WORKPLACE LEARNING
FRAMEWORK

After I completed analyzing my data, I saw an opportunity to develop a framework, which I call the SINOGAP Workplace Learning Framework. The SINOGAP Workplace Learning Framework provides a quick visual representation of how workplace learning occurs for managers.

Centre of the Framework

In the centre of the circle sits a continuum of workplace learning that ranges from unconscious to conscious levels of awareness. On the unconscious side of the continuum is implicit learning, which encompasses work processes that include, but are not limited to, collaborating with others, gaining specific job-related experience in the workplace, and problem-solving.

On the opposing end of the continuum is deliberate learning—learning activities that are purposeful, occur on a conscious level, and are mostly outside of the immediate work environment. Examples of these types of learning activities are workshops, conferences, and university courses. In the middle of the continuum is reactive learning—learning processes within work that are embedded in the many work activities (e.g., acting and seconded positions). The difference is the amount of conscious effort or awareness applied to the amount and quality of learning.

As mentioned earlier, not all experiences lend themselves to learning. The more aware or conscious we are of our learning, which occurs through moments of self-reflection, the more we learn and the more able we become to adapt and improve our performance. Therefore, self-reflection is one of the important elements of learning.

Second Layer of the Framework
The next layer of the circle includes leadership competencies, the four domains of emotional intelligence required to develop and sustain trusting relationships in the workplace. Emotions and cognitive processes are intricately linked and can drive a manager's temperament and behaviour, especially during times of high stress.

Outer Layer of the Framework
The outermost layer in the circle relates to others in the workplace who play a supportive role and enhance workplace learning. As discussed earlier, learning in the workplace depends on the relationships and support a manager receives. Although learning occurs and arises out of doing the job, it is the interactions a manager has with her colleagues, supervisors, and mentors that create opportunities for learning. For example, receiving good feedback is critical to a manager's ability to learn, because through feedback she can learn what her strengths are and how to improve her areas of weakness.

PART 3

A Call to Action

8

RECOMMENDATIONS FOR CHANGE

Some of an organization's most valuable resources are its managers; a failure to develop their competence can lead to a disengaged workforce. Therefore, the organization must develop and support expansive workplace learning strategies to develop a competent managerial workforce. Below are three key implications and three recommendations managers and C-suite leaders can implement to support leadership and managerial development.

Key Implication #1
Leadership versus Management

As I mentioned earlier, I used to believe that leadership and management were one and the same. Over the course of my research I began to understand that although they are different, each adds value to an organization's ability to achieve its goals. But nowadays who says, "I want to be a great manager?" It's all about leadership! As Gosling and Mintzberg wrote for an article in the *Harvard Business Review*, "Nobody aspires to be a good manager anymore; everybody wants to be a great leader."[49] But the separation of leadership and management has its consequences. Management without leadership can lead to a disengaged workforce, while leadership without management can lead to unachieved business goals. I am sure we all have experienced a manager who struggles to relate to others and never emerges from his office. Just as we all know a leader who is well-liked but struggles to lead projects successfully to completion.

Managers are faced with multiple dilemmas. The managers in my study expressed the importance of considering the larger system they worked within (e.g., systems thinking), while at the same time considering the needs of their employees (e.g., emotional intelligence). They spoke of having to be adaptable to continual change, while needing to maintain order and consistency. Managers have to be able to think about achieving and monitoring results, while inspiring and motivating others to have an interest and commitment to work.

Ultimately, managers have a choice. They can either choose to sit isolated in their office, which may be conducive to responding to e-mails and writing reports, or they can choose to venture beyond the walls of their office to spend time with their staff. We develop trusting relationships with people we know and share our experience with, which cannot happen behind a closed door.

Key Implication #2
Managerial Learning Happens in the Workplace, Not a Classroom

Learning how to be a manager and a leader occurs through everyday work. It is dependent on the relationships and supports we have in the workplace. Learning happens from doing the job, solving problems, coping with change, and from interactions with our staff, supervisors, mentors, and peers. While managers learn on an individual level (e.g., self-reflection), it's enhanced through the relationships they have with others (e.g., mentors). This supports research that has shown the workplace environment can either create opportunities for, or barriers to, learning.[50]

Managerial performance depends not only on confidence and commitment to the organization, but also on the value and challenge of work and the supports received in the workplace. Learning takes place in the normal course of daily work and activities, which means managers are not always consciously aware of their learning. Hence, strategies for supporting managerial learning has to include structured activities to maximize learning to its fullest potential.

There are benefits to designing structured workplace learning strategies. Learning is an active process of dealing with changing circumstances and problems through testing solutions and interacting with others. Of course, not all experience contributes to learning. In fact, some experience can prevent learning. When managers are learning, they move back and forth between reflection, action, feeling, and thinking. For an experience to contribute to learning, it requires reflection to be remembered and to influence behaviour. An experience may never become a learning moment if learning was not the intended outcome or if the experience occurred too quickly for it to be reflected upon. For instance, we usually do not have time to stop and ponder during a crisis. We need to act fast and decide what action to take to manage the situation and prevent further problems.

To improve managerial performance, managers need to reflect on their performance, to think back on what they have done to discover how their actions may have contributed to an outcome. Since managers do not easily transfer knowledge gained from a course to the job, expansive workplace learning strategies must be developed to build a strong managerial workforce. Failure to develop expansive workplace learning environments may result in restrictive work environments that can become a breeding ground for people management systems that rely on command and control, low-trust relationships, and little tolerance for making mistakes.

Key Implication #3
Equitable Succession Processes

Succession processes are a method of identifying management positions, starting at the level of a supervisor and going all the way to the highest level in the organization. Think about succession processes occurring along a continuum with replacement planning on one end and succession management on the other. Replacement planning focuses on identifying someone who can quickly backfill a vacant position on a short-term basis. It is an ad hoc process that usually involves a senior manager or mentor guiding a person he or she believes would be a good fit. In contrast, succession management is a well-thought-out process to promote people into key managerial positions, more often to retain knowledge or to encourage specific individuals to advance in their careers.

In my study, most of the secondment opportunities were long-term positions implemented through formalized succession management processes, meaning candidates had to apply and interview for the position. In contrast, acting opportunities were short-term and occurred mainly as replacement planning. The managers in my study discussed how important it was to have access to short-term acting positions when applying for long-term secondment and permanent opportunities. The learning gained from the short-term acting positions helped them gain knowledge and confidence. It also increased morale, since there were opportunities to be promoted from within.

How an organization selects, promotes, and develops their managers can have significant implications for the long-term success of an organization. Replacement planning and succession management can act as a main *feeder* for replacing positions within an organization. Hence, classroom training should not be considered as the dominant method of learning for managers. Learning happens best through on-the-job experiences. Therefore, standardized and inclusive succession processes should be developed to ensure equitable practices are implemented. This will ensure secondments and acting positions are expansive and not restrictive. For example, a potential candidate can apply and interview for future acting and secondment opportunities that are both short- and long-term. Although individuals are active participants in their own destiny, one cannot discount the important role the organization plays in creating opportunities for, or barriers to, professional growth and promotion. Therefore, I recommend three strategies that, when implemented, will increase expansive and workplace learning opportunities.

Recommendation #1
Leverage Replacement Planning and Succession Management Processes

If replacement planning and succession management are the main method for filling supervisor and manager positions within your organization, I strongly recommended that a standardized and inclusive succession and management process be developed to ensure equitable practices are followed. An example of this can be implementing a practice where individuals who are interested in moving into a supervisor or manager position go through a recruitment process that involves completing an application that communicates their aspiration, followed by participating in an interview. Successful candidates could then be eligible for short-term acting and long-term secondment opportunities.

Recommendation #2
Maximize Mentoring

My second recommendation is grounded within the concept of mentorship. As I have mentioned ad nauseum, the majority of learning that occurs in the workplace is dependent on the relationships and supports (e.g., mentors) managers have. Therefore, it is important that once an individual has been identified as a potential candidate through the succession and management process, they are assigned a mentor(s) to support their learning. Mentors should be selected based on their leadership and managerial competencies, in addition to receiving some training to develop their mentorship skills (e.g., listening, coaching, developing goals, and monitoring the achievement of goals).

Once an individual has successfully gone through the succession and management process and designated a mentor(s), it is time to focus on how their work is allocated and structured.

Recommendation #3
Restructure the Allocation of Work

For a new manager to be successful, his work needs to be challenging but not too overwhelming. Managers need to have time to engage in thoughtful reflection with their mentor so that learning from experience is more mindful and purposeful. The results from my research demonstrate that slower paced work environments are favourable to learning and ideal in building confidence. Work can be allocated in incrementally challenging duties and tasks. This is referred to as the *zone of proximal development.*[51] The zone of proximal development is the distance between an individual's *actual* ability and their *potential* ability. Through the support and guidance from others (e.g., mentors, peers, and direct reports) an individual can reach their full potential. Therefore, the zone of proximal development becomes a vehicle in which a manager's learning can be enhanced through moments of self-reflection and conversations with mentors.

When managers work in constantly hectic environments, they can become overwhelmed and struggle to maintain endurance and motivation. Unfortunately, when this occurs everyone suffers, both the team and the organization. I call this the *Sherpa Effect.* Sherpas are individuals who are highly skilled and experienced climbers. They are paid for their incredible mountaineering ability and to lead less experienced climbers through challenging and, at times, treacherous terrain. Sherpas do things such as prepare the route for climbers, secure supports, and carry heavy climbing equipment up the mountain. Sound familiar? I am sure managers reading this can relate to that experience. We just do our mountaineering in the workplace, not on Mount Everest (unless your workplace is Everest).

Climbing treacherous mountains is tough and being a Sherpa is a risky job. Being a manager is also really tough. We are exposed to risks every day. Whether that is having to fire someone we have held accountable numerous times or trying a new approach that has never been attempted before, there is a lot riding on our actions and decisions. Managers are expected to carry a heavier load than their team members. Hell, that is why I love being a manager! I like being accountable and doing things that others are too afraid to try.

I always say that being a manager is an exercise in sacrifice. We have to decide whether we will sacrifice the 300 e-mails in our inbox so we can focus on the person standing in our doorway needing our help. Or maybe we will sacrifice the briefing report that is due tomorrow morning at 9 so we can drive our daughter to hockey practice. The question I ask organizations is this, "Do we need to allocate workloads that are impossible to complete within the boundaries of assigned timelines?" Who is winning when we do that? Definitely not the manager who sacrifices the relationships with his team to get the work done. Definitely not the family who hasn't seen mom in three months, hoping that after the end of this project life will return to normal. Who are we kidding? It never does.

If the manager is not winning, nor her team, nor her family, then who is? Definitely not the organization! Then why do we keep doing the same thing only to get the same result? That is the definition of insanity. So please, let's stop the insanity! Let's actually do something different. The challenge I present to C-suite leaders is to invest in workplace learning strategies that will unlock the full potential of their managers and will enhance leadership and employee engagement at every level. Once an organization makes the commitment to invest in their people, they will begin to see their managers transform into confident and capable leaders who achieve organizational excellence and are a source of strategic value.

Time to Reflect:

1. Name one commitment you will make to enhance workplace learning in your organization.
2. How will you begin the journey?

9

WOMAN UP! IGNITE THE LEADER IN YOU

After I completed chapter eight, I thought to myself, "Yeah, I just finished my first book!" Eight chapters is a nice round number and I ended it on a bang. But then I began to reflect on my experiences as a female manager working in a male-dominated industry, law enforcement, to be exact. The challenges I faced during my leadership journey were very different than that of my male peers, as I am sure many women can relate to. I would do a disservice to all the women I know who have succeeded in spite of the challenges they faced, if I did not end my book by acknowledging a woman's unique circumstances. And as I am writing this now, Madonna's *Express Yourself* came up on my music streaming service. If that isn't a sign, I do not know what is. Now, if you are a man reading this, please read on. Male colleagues are critical to eliminating the leadership gender gap. We cannot do it without you.

Even though women are increasingly entering male-dominated professions, there is still a gender gap in formal leadership positions. Recently, I started playing in the stock market and one of the first things I research before invest-ing in a company is who sits on the board of directors and the management team. According to the *2020 Global Gap Report*,[52] boards of directors comprise only 26% women. The majority of the board of directors' positions are held by men, which is what I discovered. The same goes for the management team, except for one position. The vice presi-dent of Human Resources tends to be a woman.

Gender parity has a fundamental bearing on whether or not economies and societies thrive. Developing and de-ploying one-half of the world's available talent has a huge bearing on the growth, competitiveness, and readiness of economies and businesses worldwide. The *2017 McKinsey Global Institute Report* found that increasing gender equal-ity in the Canadian workplace could add $150 billion to the total value of goods and services produced in our country by 2026.[53]

But what does a women leader in a male-dominated industry look and feel like? I joked with a friend that I be-lieve all industries are male. I dared her to give me a tradi-tional female industry and I would demonstrate how in fact it is really male-dominated. So, she threw out education. Education, which has been traditionally female, has men occupying the top superintendent positions. A friend who is a teacher joked that the women are doing all the work, while the men are making all the decisions. So back to my question—what does a women leader in a male-dominated industry look and feel like? In my own experience, I lived between two tensions, embodying a leadership approach that felt authentic to me and embodying one that my male peers demonstrated. My leadership approach was to invest a lot in relationships. I once lent my Dr. Ho TENS machine to someone on my team because she had a sore neck. Too personal? Perhaps in some situations, but that is what feels natural to me. I care about my team and if they are not feeling well, I will do what I can to help them. I don't want them to be off work for an indefinite amount of time. Their presence and contributions are critical to the success of the team and the organization.

Leading in an Authentic Way

I distinctly remember a time when my male colleague invited me to his office. He wanted to share his concerns about one of my direct reports. He proceeded to tell me how he would have dealt with the situation and that I should follow his advice if I want to keep my team in line. My first sentiment after leaving his office was that I failed to lead my team appropriately. But that feeling was quickly replaced with frustration and anger that he had the audacity to tell me how to do my job! His observations were not observations, but assumptions of why someone on my team was behaving a certain way. And this was coming from a manager who would take calls during one-on-ones with his direct reports and would undermine them by rudely challenging everything they did. The one thing I regret is that I didn't march back into his office and tell him that his mansplaining was patronizing and inappropriate. He can lead his way and I will lead my way, thank you very much. Actually, I could have taught him a thing or two. He had high turnover in his team, whereas I did not. Proof is in the pudding, as they say. So, the lesson I learned is that leading in an authentic way means living your life according to your inner being, not someone else's.

Women cannot subscribe to someone else's vision, ideals, or philosophy of leadership. It is about defining leadership for yourself and how to embody the characteristics of a leader that you would be proud to follow. Your authentic approach to leading yourself and others has to align with your passion and purpose. I inherently believe what drives people to excellence is igniting their passion through their purpose. So, developing your authentic leadership style begins with figuring out why you want to be a formal leader in the first place.

As I mentioned in the last chapter, being a leader is tough. I am sure we all have moments where we wonder if it is worth it. Knowing why you want to lead others in the first place can help sustain you during the most challenging times. No one wants to run over a pedestrian because they are absorbed in thoughts of how they are going to manage another crazy day. Knowing what you are passionate about and how it aligns to your reason for being a leader is critical. In fact, I encourage everyone to ask that question at the next interview. Don't ask, "Why do you want this job?" Ask "Why do you want to lead others?" The response may make your decision much easier. I do not want to hire someone who says, "Well, it is the next natural progression in my career." I want someone who says, "I believe in the mission of this organization and I want to inspire others in achieving it." Damn straight! That is the person I want on my team.

Embrace your Superpowers

The next thing we need to focus on is defining our superpowers. I first heard the term superpowers in this context from a woman I admire. She had participated in the Judy Project, which is one of Canada's leading executive forums, uniquely designed to prepare women for executive and C-suite positions.[54] As part of the Judy Project, participants are asked to pay it forward and that is what she did. She brought her teachings back to her organization to share with others. During one of her seminars, she referred to a superpower as a strength someone possesses, but one that is more than just a strength. It's a strength on steroids. When you ask a woman to think of her superpower, she has to embrace what she is great at and not make excuses for it. I loved the term so much that I brought it back to my team. I told them we would spend the next several weeks exploring our superpowers. They laughed and said they forgot their capes at home. They eventually expressed that they were not comfortable thinking about themselves in that way, which cemented the importance of conducting the activity for me.

Over the next several weeks we learned things about ourselves that we had not known. We became extremely efficient and effective as a team because we reduced the amount of time we took to complete tasks. We learned who could take on certain tasks, which made my job easier. I no longer felt the pressure to have to be good at everything, because there were strong women on my team who could do things better than me. It was very empowering.

When I decided to resign from the Government of Alberta to start Sinogap Solutions, I sent out a five-question survey to people I trusted would be honest with me. I needed to explore my superpowers in more depth to build my confidence to take a huge leap of faith and quit my job as a senior manager. The questions I asked were:

1. When have you seen me thriving at my best (i.e., what was I doing or working on)?
2. What are three adjectives that best describe me?
3. What is something you think I do well?

4. What is something you think I do not do well?
5. What have you learned from me by working with me or by observing me?

The answers I received gave me so much insight into what my superpowers are and where I can still grow and develop. Knowing your strengths and areas for growth is where we all have to begin. There is a lot of self-empowerment in embracing ourselves and being proud of who we are and what we have to offer, in spite of the expectations we feel others place on us as women, mothers, sisters, friends, and colleagues. But that is not enough. There is another huge player in this story that needs to develop self-awareness and take ownership of the realities they are responsible for creating: organizations. I am speaking directly to the C-suite leaders who are reading this; the next bit is for you, so read this part with thoughtful intention.

The Organization's Role

It is important to consider the representation of women in formal leadership positions within your organization. The reality is that in many male-dominated industries it is not uncommon for women to have limited access to informal networks, influential colleagues, and mentors, which can create a barrier to upward mobility within an organization. Earlier in the book, under the section "Checking our Biases at the Door," I described a theory titled the *confidence-gap* theory. To recap, the confidence-gap theory states women have lower self-esteem than men and as a result they will avoid promoting themselves unless they are 100% sure they can do the job, whereas men will typically jump right in believing they will succeed. As I wrote earlier, I personally do not support the confidence-gap theory because it places a lot of pressure on women to carry the burden of transforming the system. Organizations need to shoulder some of the responsibility to ensure they are creating equitable workplace practices that will support women throughout their careers. As I mentioned earlier, how an organization selects, promotes, and develops their leaders can have reverberating implications for its own long-term success.

Here is one concrete example I believe you will relate to. As I discussed in chapter 8, a common practice for organizations is to promote people into acting positions to fill a short-term vacancy, which usually involves a senior manager selecting someone they believe would be a good replacement. Through those positions, women can gain tremendous experience, knowledge and confidence, things required to seek out new opportunities and take risks. An acting position also operates as an instrument for individual enlightenment and organizational learning. Executive leaders need to develop equitable and inclusive strategies that incorporate the ideas and perspectives of women if they want to create equitable succession management processes.

C-suite leaders can begin to develop more self-awareness by asking themselves three basic questions.

1. How do your beliefs influence the way your organization identifies people to develop and promote?
2. Who typically gets invited to participate in social and informal networking activities (e.g., sports tournaments, lunch or dinner outings, etc.) and/or mentoring opportunities in your organization?
3. Explain the rationale for that practice and how it may influence opportunities for advancement.

These questions may sound familiar because they appear as the self-reflection questions at the end of the section, "Checking Our Biases at the Door." The answers to those questions may reveal more than you ever considered. It could create a powerful ah-ha moment that can become the catalyst for progress and innovation that creates more equitable and inclusive practices for women in your organization. We need to uncover our biases and the only way to do that is to get feedback from the people in our company. Just be ready to hear their opinions with an open mind and heart. Don't ask for feedback if you are not willing or able to make changes. Nothing is less authentic and frustrating than that!

Rising to the Top of Your Organization

As a woman who may be exploring how to rise to the top of your organization, think about the following: What are the values of my organization? How are those values demonstrated through top leaders' behaviours? For instance, would a woman who is eight months pregnant be encouraged to apply for a promotion or ask for a raise? I challenge antiquated beliefs that when a woman leaves the workforce temporarily to raise her child, she isn't developing critical leadership skills. Isn't raising a human being to be a healthy and resilient member of society the ultimate organizational goal of humanity?

If you have the good fortune to work for an organization that has equitable processes, then begin to explore opportunities you have access to, such as mentors, coaches, and informal networking events. An important element in leadership is the ability to develop trusting bonds with other people you work with.

All the managers in my study had access to mentors and sponsors, someone who advocated for them and promoted them for special committee work that would give them access to other influential leaders and a deeper understanding of the organization. These experiences can help women by exposing them to a variety of opportunities, developing their confidence, and expanding their networks. Being selected for a special committee can be stressful, so you have to be willing to take risks. You are required to do something different and there is a chance of failure. But as women, we cannot stay in a safety zone, otherwise we will not grow and develop our superpowers to their fullest extent.

However, if you determine you do not work for an organization that has equitable practices, then you have two options. One is to stay and do your best to influence the organization to transform. If that is not feasible, then you could conclude that the organization's values do not align with your own and you may have to make the decision to work somewhere else. This also presents a lot of risk and discomfort. But what is the alternative? You could stay and see opportunities continually pass you by, or watch as less qualified and capable people get promoted and become your boss. How discouraging is that? Organizations also lose when their best talent walks out the door to work for their competitor.

The reality is that this occurs, and I am sure many women agree. This very situation happened to a close friend who had to seek opportunities outside of her immediate work environment by developing relationships and networks in other parts of her industry. This reality is the most challenging factor that women in male-dominated industries face. Part of bringing about radical transformation in practice and culture is being willing to take a stand and challenge the system. Sometimes that means rallying other like-minded people, like male allies, to start a movement with you. Like Madonna said, "Don't go for second best baby... Express yourself!"[55]

Knowing Thyself

And now we come full circle. It all starts with self-awareness, the first domain of emotional intelligence. Know your superpowers and areas for growth. Discover your passion and purpose as it relates to leadership. Your authentic approach in leading yourself and others has to align with your passion and purpose. Earlier I wrote that I inherently believe what drives people to excellence is igniting their passion through their purpose. It is also the first quote in this book. Knowing yourself is all about knowing what you are passionate about and how that influences every decision you make. So, ask yourself, "how do my passions drive me toward personal excellence?"

Being a manager myself, I have struggled with balancing my managerial duties with my leadership responsibilities. There were times throughout my career when I wondered if I were doing it right. I constantly asked myself questions such as, does my team like me, do they think I'm competent, and do they trust me? One of the key insights I gained over the years is employees do not get to choose their manager. For better or worse, employees are stuck with the manager picked for them by someone else. Leading in an authentic way means choosing to be a leader others would want to follow. So, for our last self-reflection question...

What kind of leader will you choose to be?

Woman Up! Ignite the Leader in You Program

When I started Sinogap Solutions, I wanted to create a unique learning experience for women early in their leadership journey who would like more support to develop their skill in leading others with heart and purpose. The program's mission is to help women on a leadership journey to unlock their full potential by igniting their passion through their purpose. I believe that eliminating the leadership gender gap will have a fundamental impact on an organization's ability to thrive and excel in today's agile marketplace. The outcomes of the program focus on:

- Discovering your purpose (why) for leading others.
- Uncovering the competencies required to develop your authentic leadership style.
- Leveraging existing mechanisms in your workplace to support your leadership development.
- Exploring your organization's role in creating equitable and accessible practices for selecting and promoting women.
- Developing strategies to increase your sphere of influence within your organization.

There are various options to customize your learning journey. To learn more and explore your options, visit https://sinogapsolutions.com/product/woman-up.

I wish you the very best on your leadership journey and remember—you can do anything you set your mind to. You deserve it because you earned it.

Appendix A

WHAT MANAGERS LEARN	HOW MANAGERS LEARN	WORKPLACE FACTORS THAT AFFECT LEARNING
Leadership Competencies	**Leadership Competencies Work Processes**	**Leadership Competencies Learning Factors**
• Self-awareness • Self-management • Social awareness • Relationship management	• Collaborating with others • Solving problems • Consulting others • On-the-job experiences	• Confidence and commitment • Feedback and support • Challenge and value of work
Manager Competencies	**Learning Processes**	**Context Factors**
• Systems thinking • Controlling assets • Overseeing systems and processes • Achieving and monitoring results	• Asking questions • Seeking feedback • Acting/seconded positions • Special projects and committee work	• Encounters and relationships with others at work • Allocating and structuring of work
	Learning Activities • University courses • Conferences • Workshops	

Appendix B

EXPANSIVE AND RESTRICTIVE LEARNING FACTORS

EXPANSIVE	RESTRICTIVE
Access to mentors	Little to no access to mentors
Participation in special projects	Exclusive access to participate in committees
Participation in social activities	Exclusive access to social activities
Debriefs	Little tolerance for making mistakes
Strong bonds among employees	Employees are disconnected and isolated

APPENDIX C

EXPANSIVE AND RESTRICTIVE CONTEXT FACTORS

EXPANSIVE	RESTRICTIVE
Access to acting and secondment opportunities	Limited access to acting and secondment opportunities
Equitable succession processes	Biased succession processes
Slower paced work environments	Constantly hectic work environments
Collaborative work environments	Segregated working groups

Acknowledgments

My PhD research and nearly two decades of experience in organizational development in non-profit, private, and public sectors led me to write this book. It is based on my own research and the research of other theorists whose work motivates and inspires me. I extend my thanks to the people who encouraged and supported me in the pursuit of scholarly achievement and career aspirations.

- Dr. Heather Kanuka for believing in me and knowing when I needed encouragement to move forward. You were critical in helping me believe that I had the smarts and dedication to become a scholar.
- Carol Arnold-Schutta for supporting and encouraging me throughout this long journey. You not only gave me the gift of time to conduct my research, you also promoted my work by encouraging me to integrate it into all of the leadership programs we designed and implemented.
- The theorists who forged the path before me and who continue to motivate me to stay curious.
- Most importantly, the participants and the leaders throughout my career who volunteered their time and shared their stories with me. You inspire me to be a strong leader and a better manager.

CITATIONS

A Note from Johanna

1   Eraut, M. (2004). *Informal learning in the workplace: Studies in Continuing Education*, 26(2), 247–273.
2   Mintzberg, H. (1989). *On Management*. New York: Free Press.
3   Mintzberg, H. (2013). *Simply Managing: What Managers Do – and Can Do Better*. San Francisco, CA: Berrett-Koehler.
4   Schön, D. A. (1987). *Educating the reflective practitioner*. San Francisco, CA: Josey-Bass Inc.
5   Cook, C.W., Hunsaker, P.L., & Coffey, R. E. (1997). *Management and Organizational Behavior*. Chicago: Irwin.

Checking our Biases at the Door

6   Global Education Monitoring Report (2017, October). Retrieved from https://gem-report-2017.unesco.org/en/chapter/gender_monitoring_leadership/
7   Fuller, A. and Unwin, L. (2006). Expansive and restrictive learning environments. In K. Evans, P. Hodkinson, H. Rainbird, and L. Unwin, *Improving workplace learning* (pp. 27–48). London: Routledge.
8   World Economic Forum (2020). *The Global Gender Gap*. Retrieved from https://www.weforum.org/reports/gender-gap-2020-report-100-years-pay-equality.
9   Gallup. Why Managers Are Central to an Agile Culture (2018, October 10). Retrieved from https://www.gallup.com/workplace/243455/why-managers-central-agile-culture.aspx.

[10] Berke, D., & Center for Creative Leadership. (2005). *Succession planning and management: A Guide to Organizational Systems and Practices.* Greensboro, N.C.: Center for Creative Leadership.

[11] Rothwell, W. J., (2001). *Effective succession planning.* New York, NY: AMACOM American Management Association.

[12] Statistics Canada. Women and Paid Work. (2017, March 9). Retrieved from https://www150.statcan.gc.ca/n1/pub/89-503-x/2015001/article/14694-eng.htm

[14] Zenger Folkman. The Impact of Women Leaders (2015, March 6). (Webinar). Retrieved from https://zengerfolkman.com/webinars/the-impact-of-women-leaders/

[15] *Harvard Business Review.* Is the Confidence Gap Between Men and Women a Myth? (2018, March 26). Retrieved from https://hbr.org/2018/03/is-the-confidence-gap-between-men-and-women-a-myth.

[16] Lave, J. & Wenger, E. (1991). *Situated learning.* Cambridge: Cambridge University Press.
Evans, K. & Rainbird, H. (2006). Workplace learning: Perspectives and challenges. In K. Evans, P. Hodkinson, H. Rainbird, & L. Unwin (Eds.), *Improving workplace learning* (pp. 1-23). London: Routledge.

[17] Eraut, M. (2007). Learning from other people in the workplace. *Oxford Review of Education,* 33(4), 403-422.

[18] Eraut, M. (2012). Developing a broader approach to professional learning. In A. McKee & M. Eraut (Eds.), *Learning Trajectories, Innovation and Identity for Professional Development, volume 7* (pp. 21-46). New York: Springer. Marsick, V. J., & Watkins, K. E. (1990). *Informal and Incidental Learning in the*

Workplace. New York: Routledge. Wenger, E. (1998). *Communities of Practice: Learning, Meaning and Identity.* Cambridge, UK: Cambridge University Press.

[19] Robinson, K. (2013, April). How to escape education's death valley (Video file). Retrieved from https://www.ted.com/talks/ken_robinson_how_to_escape_education_s_death_valley.

Chapter 1: Mind the Gap

[20] Mabey, C. (2008). Management development and firm performance in Germany, Norway, Spain and the UK. *Journal of International Business Studies*, 39(8), 1327-1342.

[21] 2019 Training Industry Report. Retrieved from https://trainingmag.com/trgmag-article/2019-training-industry-report/

[22] Building a Learning Organization (1993, July-August). Retrieved from https://hbr.org/1993/07/building-a-learning-organization.

[23] Marsick, V. J. (2003). Invited reaction: Informal learning and the transfer of learning: How managers develop proficiency. *Human Resource Development Quarterly*, 14(4), 389-395.

[24] The End of the Traditional Manager. (2018, May). Retrieved from https://www.gallup.com/workplace/235811/end-traditional-manager.aspx.

[25] Evans, K. & Rainbird, H. (2006). Workplace learning: Perspectives and challenges. In K. Evans, P. Hodkinson, H. Rainbird, & L. Unwin (Eds.), *Improving workplace learning* (pp. 1-23). London: Routledge.

Chapter 2: The Nature of Informal Learning

[26] Davenport, T.O. & Harding, S. D. (2010). *Manager Redefined*. San Francisco, CA: Jossey-Bass.

[27] Eraut, M. (2004). *Informal learning in the workplace: Studies in Continuing Education*, 26(2), 247–273. Eraut, M. (2007). Learning from other people in the workplace. *Oxford Review of Education*, 33(4), 403-422. Garrick, J. (1998). *Informal Learning in the Workplace: Unmasking Human Resource Development*. New York: Routledge. Marsick, V. J., & Watkins, K. E. (1990). *Informal and Incidental Learning in the Workplace*. New York: Routledge.

[28] Dewey, J. (1938). *Experience and Education*. New York: The Macmillan Co.

[29] Kolb, A., & Kolb, D. A. (2005). *Experiential learning theory bibliography*. Cleveland, OH: Experience Based Learning Systems, Inc., p.194.

[30] Schön, D. A. (1987). *Educating the Reflective Practitioner*. San Francisco, CA: Josey-Bass Inc.

[31] Schmidt, H. G., & Boshuizen, H. A. (1993). On acquiring expertise in medicine. *Educational Psychology Review*, (3) 205-221.

Chapter 3: Why Training Fails

[32] Crotty, M. (1998). *The Foundations of Social Research: Meaning and Perspective in the Research Process*. Thousand Oaks, CA: SAGE.

[33] Hager, P. (2011). Theories of Workplace Learning. In M. Malloch, L. Cairns, K. Evans & B.N. O'Connor (Eds.), The SAGE Handbook of Workplace Learning (pp. 443-466). Retrieved from http://dx.doi.org/10.4135/9781446200940.n2

34   Reiser, R.A. & Dempsey, J.V. (2012). *Trends and Issues in Instructional Design and Technology* (2nd Ed.). Upper Saddle River, NJ: Pearson Education.

35   Eraut, M. (2004). *Informal learning in the workplace: Studies in Continuing Education*, 26(2), 247–273.
     Evans, K. & Rainbird, H. (2006). Workplace learning: Perspectives and challenges. In K. Evans, P. Hodkinson, H. Rainbird, & L. Unwin (Eds.), *Improving workplace learning* (pp. 1-23). London: Routledge.

36   Evans, K. & Rainbird, H. (2006). Workplace learning: Perspectives and challenges. In K. Evans, P. Hodkinson, H. Rainbird, & L. Unwin (Eds.), *Improving workplace learning* (pp. 1-23). London: Routledge.

37   Eraut, M. (2004). *Informal learning in the workplace: Studies in Continuing Education*, 26(2), 247–273 p. 256

38   The #1 Reason Leadership Development Fails. (2012, Dec 19). Retrieved from https://www.forbes.com/sites/mikemyatt/2012/12/19/the-1-reason-leadership-development-fails/#22a8a7396522

Chapter 4: What Managers Learn

39   Goleman, D., Boyatzis, R., & McKee, A. (2002). *Primal leadership.* Boston, Massachusetts: Harvard Business School Press.

40   Boyatzis R., & McKee, A. (2005). *Resonant Leadership.* Boston, Massachusetts: Harvard Business School Press.

41   Kouzes, J. M., & Posner, B. Z. (2007). *The Leadership Challenge*, 4th ed. San Francisco, CA: Jossey-Bass.

42   Lencioni, P. (2012). *The Advantage. Why Organizational Health Trumps Everything Else in Business.* San Francisco, C: Jossey-Bass.

[43] Cook, C.W., Hunsaker, P.L., & Coffey, R. E. (1997). *Management and Organizational Behavior*. Chicago: Irwin.

Chapter 5: How Managers Learn Through Everyday Work

[44] Eraut, M. (2004). Informal learning in the workplace. *Studies in Continuing Education*, 26(2), 247–273, p. 406.

[45] Eraut, M. (2007). Learning from other people in the workplace. *Oxford Review of Education*, 33(4), 403-422.

Chapter 6: Workplace Factors that Enable and Impede Managerial Learning

[46] Engeström, 2001; Eraut, 2007; Fuller & Unwin, 2006; Lave & Wenger, 1991.

[47] Eraut, M. (2007). Learning from other people in the workplace. *Oxford Review of Education*, *33*(4), 403-422.

[48] Fuller, A. and Unwin, L. (2006). Expansive and restrictive learning environments. In K. Evans, P. Hodkinson, H. Rainbird, and L. Unwin, *Improving workplace learning* (pp. 27–48). London: Routledge.

Chapter 8: Recommendations for Change

[49] Gosling, J., & Mintzberg, H. (2003). The Five Minds of a Manager. *Harvard Business Review*, *81*(11), 54-63. p. 54

[50] Eraut, M. (2007). Learning from other people in the workplace. *Oxford Review of Education*, *33*(4), 403-422. Fuller, A. and Unwin, L. (2006). Expansive and restrictive learning environments. In K. Evans, P. Hodkinson, H. Rainbird, and L. Unwin, *Improving workplace learning* (pp. 27–48). London: Routledge.

[51] Kolb, D. A. (2015). *Experiential Learning: Experience as the Source of Learning and Development* (2nd ed.). New Jersey: Pearson Education Inc.

Chapter 9: Woman Up! Ignite the Leader in You

[52] World Economic Forum (2020). *The Global Gender Gap.* Retrievedfromhttps://www.weforum.org/reports/gender-gap-2020-report-100-years-pay-equality

[53] *2017 McKinsey Global Institute Report.* Retrieved from https://www.mckinsey.com/featured-insights/gender-equality/the-power-of-parity-advancing-womens-equality-in-canada.

[54] The Judy Project. Retrieved from https://www.rotman.utoronto.ca/ProfessionalDevelopment/InitiativeFor WomenInBusiness/Programs/Judy-Project/Judy-Project-Application.

[55] "Express Yourself," *Like a Prayer* (1989, Sire Records, Warner Bros.)

Index

Made in the USA
San Bernardino, CA
26 June 2020